# 100
# FOLK HEROES
## WHO SHAPED WORLD HISTORY

Sarah Krall

A Bluewood Book

Published in 1995 by
Bluewood Books
A Division of The Siyeh Group, Inc.,
P.O. Box 460313
San Francisco, CA 94146

ISBN 0-912517-18-2

Printed in the USA

Edited by Bill Yenne

Designed and captioned by
Ruth DeJauregui

Illustrated by Tony Chikes

About the author:
**Sarah Krall** graduated from New York University and worked as a journalist before entering the publishing field as a writer and editor. She currently lives in San Francisco with her cat. This is her first book.

# TABLE OF CONTENTS

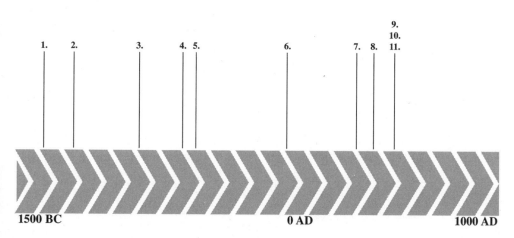

1.    2.          3.        4. 5.              6.              7.  8.  9.
                                                                      10.
                                                                      11.

1500 BC                                        0 AD              1000 AD

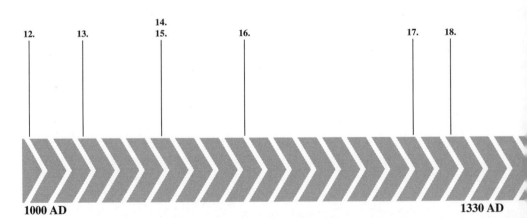

12.  13.  14. 15.  16.  17.  18.

1000 AD                                                1330 AD

**52.** JUDGE ROY BEAN  *59*
c. 1825-1903
**53.** GERONIMO  *60*
1829-1909
**54.** WILD BILL HICKOK  *61*
1832-1876
**55.** HORATIO ALGER  *62*
1832-1899
**56.** MARK TWAIN  *63*
1835-1910
**57.** GENERAL TOM THUMB  *64*
1838-1883
**58.** GEORGE ARMSTRONG CUSTER  *65*
1839-1876
**59.** JOHN HENRY  *66*
c. 1840-1871?
**60.** SARAH BERNHARDT  *67*
1844-1923
**61.** BUFFALO BILL CODY  *68*
1846-1917
**62.** JESSE JAMES  *69*
1847-1882
**63.** WYATT EARP  *70*
1848-1929
**64.** BELLE STARR  *71*
1848-1889

**65.** CALAMITY JANE  *72*
c. 1852-1903
**66.** DIAMOND JIM BRADY  *73*
1856-1917
**67.** BILLY THE KID  *74*
1859-1881
**68.** ANNIE OAKLEY  *75*
1860-1926
**69.** THE ELEPHANT MAN  *76*
1862-1890
**70.** CASEY JONES  *77*
c. 1863-1900
**71.** NELLIE BLY  *78*
c. 1867-1922
**72.** TYPHOID MARY  *79*
c. 1870-1938
**73.** RASPUTIN  *80*
c. 1871-1916
**74.** ENRICO CARUSO  *81*
1873-1921
**75.** HARRY HOUDINI  *82*
1874-1926
**76.** MATA HARI  *83*
1876-1917
**77.** PANCHO VILLA  *84*
c. 1878-1923

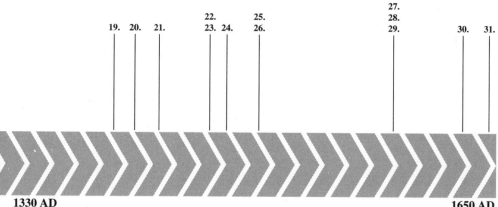

1330 AD

1650 AD

5

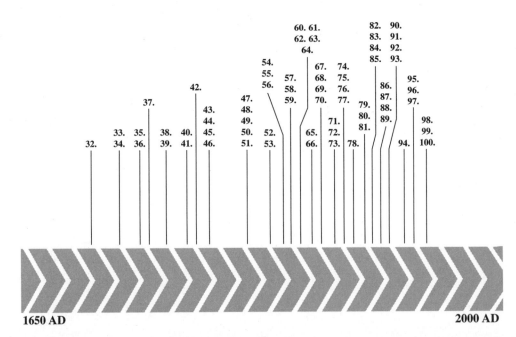

1650 AD                                                        2000 AD

# INTRODUCTION

A folk hero can be defined as anyone at the center of a much-told legend. The term "Folks" is often thought to refer to rural dwellers, but it can mean any group of people that has a common feature, whether it is occupation or nationality.

Here are 100 entries that document civilization's most immortal mortals. They represent different things to different individuals, and they can be interpreted historically, psychologically, literally, or symbolically. Although their powerful sagas have gone from being sung by bards to being images on TV and movie screens, much of their contents remain the same. The rags-to riches theme was introduced by **Horatio Alger** and applies to notables from **Diamond Jim Brady** to **Elvis Presley**. The **Robin Hood** motif — that of stealing from the rich to give the poor — also appears time and time again. It forms the basis of Wild West outlaw tradition, which has the added element of the hero's assassination being unfailingly caused by a treacherous comrade. So compelling is this mold that the motives and characters of **Billy the Kid** and **Bonnie and Clyde** were completely misrepresented in order to fit it.

This disparity between popular image and truth is most obvious in the case of **Mata Hari**, whose glamourous myth ended up distorting the human. This is because she is far more exciting as the greatest and most seductive spy ever than the bumbling amateur she apparently was.

The public has always craved scandal and mystery, and there's nothing like a tragic death to spice things up. **Marilyn Monroe** fits into all these categories, and her enduring magnetism is illustrated by the wide-ranging cultural domination of her image.

And the passage of a century has done nothing to lessen the appeal of the desperado **Jesse James**. As this book goes to press, what is generally accepted to be his corpse is being exhumed so that his true fate may become clear.

People especially love juicy gossip about a hero, especially when revealed after his or her death. **J. Edgar Hoover** and **Walt Disney** have been posthumously accused of doing many less than admirable things, but this only enhances their mystique.

Other entries describe the fascinating feats of our saints, the triumphs of our most dazzling performers, and the adventures of our bravest warriors and pioneers. What they all share is a certain indefinable quality that goes beyond their beauty, talent, personalities and actions. This special something made the masses revere them and simply admire others like them. These folk heroes left the world somehow altered, and their names will never be forgotten.

# KING TUTANKHAMEN
## c. 1358-1339 BC

**King Tutankhamen.**

Despite the fact that this boy king was historically one of ancient Egypt's least important pharaohs, **King Tutankhamen**'s magnificent tomb, the most intact and revealing of its kind, gave him such intense fame after its 1922 discovery, and again in the 1970s, when many of its contents toured Britain and America, that he has become today's archetypical pharaoh. During his first wave of popularity, his gold death mask became as familiar as the **Mona Lisa** (see no. 24), while during his second, the intense merchandising that glutted America even inspired a Top 40 song by comedian **Steve Martin**.

The British archeologist **Howard Carter** searched the **Valley of the Kings** for about a decade to find the tomb's entrance, which had gone undisturbed for over 3,000 years because it was so well camouflaged with rock chips from a nearby tomb. The tomb's exquisite treasures, which numbered over 5,000 and were intended to serve Tutankhamen in his afterlife, were crammed into three rooms and included a gold-encrusted throne, disassembled chariots, weapons, games, clothing, furniture and wine. Inside the fourth room, the burial chamber, four immense funeral canopies held a quartzite sarcophagus in which were three richly ornamented coffins; the innermost was of solid gold and held Tutankhamen's mummy, which was adorned with his bejeweled headdress, hands of sheet gold, and much gold jewelry.

Many Egyptians have always believed that pharaohs cursed their tombs for protection against intruders. "Death comes on wings to he who enters the tomb of a pharaoh," goes an Arabic proverb, while a lamp in Tutankhamen's tomb has hieroglyphs that read, "It is I who protect the dead." Misfortunes did indeed occur after the tomb's discovery. First, Carter's canary was eaten by a poisonous desert snake. Then **Lord Carnarvon**, Carter's financier, died just a few months after entering the tomb. At the moment he died, lights went out all over Cairo, and in England his favorite dog howled and dropped dead. Carnarvon's bizarre cause of death, an infected mosquito bite on his left cheek that developed into pneumonia, seemed even stranger when the mummy was unwrapped a few years later and had a wound on the same spot. Finally, Carter encountered problems with Egyptian officials, who at one point resealed the tomb.

Sherlock Holmes' creator, Sir **Arthur Conan Doyle**, gave the curse some credibility when he said he believed the lord died from "elementals — not souls, not spirits — created by Tutankhamen's priests." Newspapers viewed the demise of anyone remotely connected with the tomb as further proof of the curse, while several monster movies scripted around a mummy's curse captivated audiences. Carter disbelieved all talk of curses and did not die until 1939, at the age of 65.

The religion of King Tut, as he has been affectionately dubbed, believed that if a name was remembered and repeated posthumously, the person would have a long afterlife. If that is so, Tutankhamen still enjoys his today.

# HELEN OF TROY
## c. 1200-1150 BC

Her role in the *Iliad* (see no. 3) as the prime cause of the **Trojan War** has caused the dazzling **Helen of Troy** to represent the embodiment of those enchanting female qualities that drive men to fight and even kill. Although her existence — and indeed, the entire occurrence of the Trojan War — has been doubted, archeological excavations have decisively placed the ancient city of Troy (or Ilium) in northwestern Turkey, near the southern end of the Dardanelles.

The reverence the ancient Greeks regarded Helen with left her life recorded as an action-packed myth, complete with many different versions from the moment of her conception. As a result, a mix of a few facts with much fiction is all we know of her.

**Zeus**, the king of the gods, either visited her mortal mother **Leda** in the form of a swan or else mated with **Nemesis**, the goddess of fate. In both versions, Helen hatched from a swan's egg. While she was still a child, the Athenian hero **Theseus** fell under her spell and kidnapped her, but she was rescued by her brothers.

Later, Helen's renowned looks attracted a horde of noble but antagonistic suitors, including **Ulysses** (or **Odysseus**), who obliged each to support the one she chose. Helen selected **Menelaus**, the king of Sparta, but she was either seduced or abducted by the Trojan prince **Paris**. According to one legend, later dramatized in **Euripides'** *Helen*, the couple got as far as Egypt, where Helen remained as a guest of King **Proteus**, sending a phantom of herself to Troy.

Nevertheless, her former suitors banded together and won the ten-year-long **Trojan War** in about 1184 BC, after which Helen was reunited with Menelaus. Some chronicles say that after Menelaus' death she was exiled to Rhodes, where she was either hanged or murdered.

Whether regarded as a victim of her passions or her beauty, Helen, with her "face that launched a thousand ships," a famous phrase penned by **Christopher Marlowe** in *Doctor Faustus*, has an ageless mystique that guarantees her legend will never be forgotten.

Helen of Troy.

# HOMER
## c. 850 BC

**Homer** is believed by most to have composed the splendidly written epics the *Iliad* and the *Odyssey*, which provide us with much of what we know of Hellenistic mythology, culture and history. Perhaps his most important contribution to our cultural fabric is his vivid characters, from the man-eating **Cyclops**, to the femme fatale **Helen of Troy** (see no. 2), to the numerous immature gods and goddesses. Homer gave the epic tradition most of its conventions, including dactylic hexameter, heavy use of similes and epithets and larger-than-life speeches, omens and battle scenes. His work inspired both the form and content of great writers throughout the ages, including **Aeschylus**, **Virgil**, **Dante**, **Boccaccio**, **Chaucer**, **Goethe**, Lord **Alfred Tennyson**, **James Joyce** and **Ezra Pound**.

Homer.

Homer was not just a writer, however, but a bard, a singing poet, who probably performed or competed with others at religious festivals and noblemen's feasts, both of which may have lasted for days or even weeks. It is generally accepted that Homer was blind and recited his long tales from memory. While he may have had a scribe, a group of bards called the **Homeridae**, some of whom claimed direct descent from their namesake, may have passed the tales down from father to son and eventually recorded them, but not before elements from later times were added.

Little is known of his life and personality, although Homer may have been born in Smyrna and lived in Chios. Several ancient biographies were written, and while they are interesting, most of their facts are too fantastic to be believable. For example, one cites his original name as **Melesigenes**, a combination of those of his father, the river **Meles**, and his mother, the nymph **Crethees**. Yet another claims he was descended from **Orpheus**, an ancient poet and musician whose music was said to move inanimate objects.

# AESOP
## c. 620-565 BC

For generations, **Aesop**'s fables, with their all-too-human animal characters in allegorical situations, have been learned by most people in early childhood, whether at bedtime, in school, or even in **Bugs Bunny** cartoons. Despite all their reinterpretations, the animal fables still retain their simplistic, humorous charm. The tales of others, like **Mother Goose** (see no. 32), the brothers **Grimm** (see no. 45), and **Hans Christian Andersen** (see no. 47), also have a lasting effect on children, but Aesop's fables were the first of their kind.

Many of his stories are believed to have originated as far back as prehistoric times, meaning Aesop possibly transformed the protagonists into animals.

Like **Homer**'s epics (see no. 3), the stories are believed to have circulated orally until they were recorded in about 300 BC. In Hellenistic times, schoolboys studied his tales, and orators and philosophers used them to illustrate a point.

Each fable contains a cautionary, ageless moral. "The Tortoise and the Hare" teaches that perseverance can be more valuable than skill, while "The Ant and the Grasshopper" illustrates that diligence has life-sustaining rewards.

The fables have also given us several popular expressions. From "The Fox and the Grapes" comes the regretful phrase "sour grapes." In another fable, a wolf disguises himself as a sheep to get into the meadow where the flock grazes, giving rise to the expression "a wolf in sheep's clothing" regarding deceit.

Ancient mythical stories portrayed this liberated slave from Phyrygia as a wise, hump-backed buffoon who associated with such famed contemporaries as King **Croesus of Lydia**, the courtesan **Rhodopis**, **Solon the Athenian** lawgiver, and the **Seven Wise Men.** He is reputed to have died at the hands of the citizens of Delphi, who were insulted when he said that their celebrated oracle enabled them to profit from mankind's misfortunes. The Delphians vindictively planted a sacred golden bowl in his luggage, judged him a thief, and threw him from a cliff.

Aesop.

# 5. CONFUCIUS (KUNG FU TZU)
## c. 551-479 BC

In life **Confucius** was a humble teacher and idealistic reformer, but in death he has had so much influence in China that for the past 2,000 years, he has been their Supreme Sage and Foremost Teacher, and his name is the Latinized form of the title **Kung Fu Tzu** (or "**Kongfuzi**"), meaning "**Grand Master Kung**." His ideas, known as **Confucianism** and mostly recorded in the form of sayings, have affected Chinese education and government as well as Korean, Japanese and Vietnamese thought. While some consider Confucianism a religion, and indeed Confucius was deified after his death, every temple dedicated to him in China's some 2,000 counties has no clergy, and Confucius himself never mentioned the existence of any God or gods or life after death.

Born to an impoverished noble family in the duchy of Lu in today's Shantung province, he was originally named **Ch'iu**, meaning hill, because of a prominent bump on his head. Growing so tall that he acquired the nickname "long fellow," at age 15 the sage became interested in learning, with the ultimate goal of restoring order to Chinese society. China at that point had fallen into chaos, with never-ending warfare between states and a declining respect for established behavioral codes.

At 25, Confucius began teaching, and eventually attracted 3,000 disciples. His ideas focused on a noble character regardless of one's station, and his teaching methods were mostly relaxed conversations with individuals or small groups.

One of his well known sayings, "In education there are no class differences," illustrates the radical nature of his school, which differed from others in that admission was not restricted to the aristocracy. His teaching career was broken up by a short stint as a high minister of Lu and a 13-year sojourn throughout China.

Largely unknown when he died, Confucius' pupils spread his teachings, which achieved widespread recognition in about 100 BC. While Confucius is not believed to have left any writings, his followers compiled his teachings and sayings. These are known as the *Four Books* and the *Five Classics*, and for centuries they have been the central primary and secondary educational texts in China. In the Western world, many people say "Confucius say" before spouting any time-worn piece of advice, while fortune cookies jokingly attribute silly sayings to him.

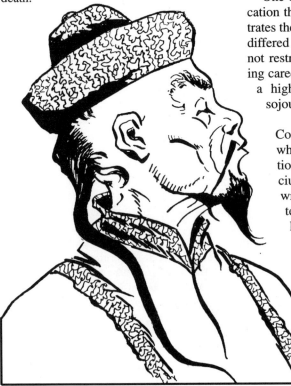

**Confucius.**

# 6. CLEOPATRA
## 69-30 BC

The alluring **Cleopatra** has become legendary because of her love affairs with the Roman leaders **Gaius Julius Caesar** (100-44 BC) and **Marcus Antonius (Mark Antony, 82-30 BC)**. Her reputation is still colored by the Romans' intense dislike for her, first conveyed by the poets **Virgil** and **Horace**, who portrayed her as a ruthless, sex-mad "wild queen" who plotted "ruin to the empire."

After Cleopatra was exiled from Alexandria by her co-ruler and brother **Ptolemy XII**, she secretly returned to the capital to secure Caesar's support with her abundant charm and wit. It worked: not only did he become enamored of her, he won a war against her brother, reinstating her to the throne with her youngest brother, **Ptolemy XIV**, as Egyptian tradition required. She returned to Rome with Augustus, who gave her and their son **Caesarion** an extravagant villa and offended his countrymen by having a golden statue of her built in the temple of **Venus Genetrix**.

Cleopatra.

After Augustus' assassination, Cleopatra returned to her kingdom and allegedly poisoned her brother so Caesarion could rule with her as **Ptolemy XV**. Shortly after this, her tragic affair with Mark Antony began. During one sumptuous banquet she prepared in his honor, she made one of history's most extraordinary and memorable love offerings by dropping two priceless pearls in her wine and drinking it after toasting his health. He, in turn, gave her and their twins the gifts of Cyprus, Phoenicia, Coele-Syria and parts of Arabia, Cilicia and Judea. This outraged the Romans, especially Antony's co-ruler **Augustus** (**Gaius Octavian**, 63 BC-14 AD), whose sister was bigamously married to Antony.

Octavian declared war against them, and after a miserable defeat at Actium, the lovers fled to Alexandria. Octavian followed them, and Cleopatra started a rumor that she had committed suicide. Antony heard it and stabbed himself in grief before learning it was untrue. He was carried to the queen, and he died in her arms. Octavian took Cleopatra prisoner and planned to exhibit her in Rome, but she killed herself first. According to legend, she died of an asp bite after her supporters smuggled the snake to her in a basket of figs.

Cleopatra's mentions in plays, literature and historical texts are countless, but her biggest tributes are the **Shakespearian tragedy** *Antony and Cleopatra* (1607) and the epic **MGM** film *Cleopatra* (1963), which starred **Elizabeth Taylor** and **Richard Burton**.

# SAINT NICHOLAS
## Early fourth century

**Saint Nicholas** inspired, and has become synonymous with, today's image of **Santa Claus**, the rotund, bearded man in red whose Christmas Eve visits are anticipated by children for months before the actual event. Children grow up believing that he travels the world on a reindeer-pulled sleigh, sliding down chimneys and leaving presents for good children.

Little is known about the life of the actual Saint Nicholas, who was the **Bishop of Myra**, located in Lycia on the coast of Asia Minor in what is now Turkey. Two famous legends are attributed to him. In the first, he restored life to three murdered boys, while in the second, he saved three maidens, who, because their father could not provide dowries, were destined for prostitution. On three successive nights, Nicholas dropped bags of gold coins into their window, enabling them to marry.

Much of Europe still celebrates December 5th, Saint Nicholas Eve, as well as December 6th, the day he supposedly died, and the saint evolved into **Father Christmas** in Germany and Protestant Europe. During the seventeenth century, Dutch settlers took their legend of **Sinter-Klaas** with them to New Amsterdam (now New York City's borough of Manhattan). Today's popular image of Santa Claus — whose name is now used interchangeably with that of Saint Nicholas — is almost entirely the creation of two men. They are **Clement C. Moore**, who wrote *A Visit from St. Nicholas* (1823), and **Thomas Nast**, whose nineteenth century illustrations of Santa Claus are still reproduced today. They popularized and expanded on his legend, making him the jolly patron of America's Christmas.

**Saint Nicholas.**

# SAINT PATRICK
### 389-461

As the patron saint of Ireland, his feast day, March 17th, is celebrated throughout the world by Irish Catholics and their descendants, who credit **Saint Patrick** with being chiefly responsible for converting Ireland to **Christianity**. This founder of over 300 churches and baptizer of over 120,000 people is said to have driven the snakes from Ireland and turned a child's tears to gems. Saint Patrick also explained the **Trinity** with a three-leaf shamrock, which many believe became Ireland's symbol as a result.

Born in Britain, Patrick was kidnapped at age 16 by pirates, who sold him into slavery in Ireland. After six years of captivity, he escaped and walked 200 Roman miles to a ship. When the ship landed in desolate country and the crew desperately wandered for three days, Patrick averted starvation when a herd of wild pigs appeared in answer to his prayers.

Once back in his native land, Patrick had a dream in which he received a letter, whose opening words were "the voice of the Irish." As he read it, he heard voices saying, "We beseech thee holy youth to come and walk once more among us." Pope Celestine I eventually approved, and in 432 the missionary began his legendary work, remaining in Ireland until his death. Saint Patrick was said to have once preached for three days and three nights without pause, but to his audience it seemed like only an hour.

**Saint Patrick.**

# KING ARTHUR and GUINEVERE
## Sixth century

Countless writers have documented the marvelous legends of this possibly-fictional Anglo-Saxon royal couple. Their very names invoke the medieval age of chivalry, in which armored knights rescued damsels in distress and the forests teemed with evil witches and sorcerers, dragons and wild beasts. **King Arthur** is famed for bringing order to this dangerous world through his brave deeds, his virtuous nature, and his establishment of the knights of the **Round Table**.

Like many other folk heroes, the obviously heavy additions of fanciful elements to the stories of King Arthur and his court have raised many questions about whether any of them ever lived. But it is known that shortly after a real king named Arthur died, the tales about him that circulated orally were already bordering upon the mythical.

According to lore, King **Uther Pendragon** was in love with the Duke of Cornwall's wife, so **Merlin**, a Celtic magician, gave Uther the duke's form and Arthur was conceived. Arthur grew up unaware of his royal ancestry, but he became king after he pulled the magic sword **Excalibur** from a block of stone. After marrying the beautiful princess **Guinevere**, Arthur waged war against the Roman emperor **Lucius**, conquering much of Western Europe. When Arthur returned to his castle at **Camelot**, he and 150 knights undertook the quest for the **Holy Grail** (see no. 11).

When the king later discovered that Guinevere and Sir **Lancelot** (see no. 10) were having an affair, the knight and queen fled. Later, Guinevere came back, and Arthur pursued Lancelot, but returned to Camelot after **Mordred**, a knight who was either Arthur's nephew or son, seized both the kingdom and its queen. Arthur killed Mordred, but died from the wounds he sustained, and the guilty Guinevere lived the rest of her life as a nun. As late as 1155, people believed that he would return any minute from the otherworldly island of **Avalon**, where he had gone to heal, and restore peace and harmony.

The early Latin, Celtic and French accounts that documented Arthur's life were used as sources for later stories, the most popular of which are Sir **Thomas Malory**'s *Le Morte d'Arthur* (c. 1470) and Lord **Alfred Tennyson**'s *Idylls of the King* (sections first appeared in 1842). More recently, films like *Camelot* (1967), *Excalibur* (1981), and *First Knight* (1995) have dazzled audiences.

**King Arthur and Guinevere.**

# 10. SIR LANCELOT
## Sixth century

A fearless and skillful warrior, Sir **Lancelot** of the Lake was King **Arthur's** favorite knight until his famous affair with Queen **Guinevere** contributed to the **Round Table's** dissolution (see no. 9). The scandalous liaison is a dominant theme in **Tennyson's** *Idylls of the King* and **Malory's** *Le Morte d'Arthur*, as well as the basis of numerous other romances.

Lancelot (or Launcelot) was the son of the king of Brittany, but the magical **Lady of the Lake** took Lancelot as an infant to her castle at the bottom of a lake and then to Arthur's court when he reached manhood. She would remain Lancelot's guardian angel throughout his life, often helping him out of dangerous situations. A brief fling with the princess **Elaine of Astolat** produced Sir **Galahad** (see no. 11). Elaine later died of her love for the handsome Lancelot. While Lancelot was part of the quest for the **Holy Grail**, he was not morally perfect enough to find it.

Later, when Arthur discovered the knight's affair with Guinevere, the lovers fled to Lancelot's castle, **Joyous Garde**. Lancelot also killed several fellow knights who discovered the romance. Eventually Lancelot returned Guinevere to **Camelot** and fled to France. After King Arthur's death, Lancelot returned to Britain, and learned that Guinevere had become a nun. He became a religious hermit, and died shortly after the queen.

Another legend has Lancelot briefly taking the throne, and then being slain by **Mordred** (see no. 9) who, according to this account, survived the last battle of King Arthur.

**Sir Lancelot.**

17

The illegitimate son of Sir **Lancelot** (see no. 10), Sir **Galahad** was the most noble and virtuous of all the knights of the **Round Table**. In Lord **Alfred Tennyson**'s *Idylls of the King*, he says, "My strength is as the strength of ten/ Because my heart is pure."

His legend relates primarily to the quest for the **Holy Grail**, which is said to have been used by **Jesus** at the **Last Supper** and by **Joseph of Arimathea** to catch Jesus' blood after he was crucified. Later, when Joseph was imprisoned, the food-producing vessel appeared and fed him for 42 years.

Galahad, said to be Joseph's last descendant, was among the many knights who witnessed the brief vision of the Grail that inspired the search. After many adventures over several years, it became clear that only Galahad and two other knights, **Bors** and **Percival**, were faultless enough to find it.

The knights went to the **Castle Corbenic**, where Joseph had taken the Grail. The unhealed wound of **Pelles**, the ruler there, precluded him from fathering children and the land around the castle from growing vegetation. Once inside, the three knights saw a vision where Joseph was a priest, and then angels brought in the Grail and a spear from the **Crucifixion** with Jesus' blood on it. A child who appeared above the Grail transformed into a loaf of bread, and Jesus materialized from the Grail to give the knights Communion. Their experience was intended to show that in Mass, the bread and wine become the body and blood of Christ.

Galahad healed Pelles with the spear's blood, after which the wound disappeared and both Pelles and the land became fertile. The three then sailed on a ship, which turned out to have the Grail aboard and was led by mystical powers to the far-off city of Sarras. After Galahad died, Bors and Percival witnessed the Grail rise into heaven, and it has not been seen since.

**Sir Galahad.**

This English countess is legendary for her naked ride on horseback through **Coventry**, a town in central England. A parade in homage to her, called the **Godiva Procession**, has been held every seven or eight years since 1678 as part of the Coventry Fair. Variations of her legend have been frequently mentioned throughout the ages in literature, poetry, painting and music.

The earliest source of her story is the *Chronica* (1057) by **Richard of Wendover**. According to the tale, **Lady Godiva** made incessant pleas to her husband **Leofric**, the Earl of Mercia or Leicester, to reduce Coventry's heavy taxes. Aggravated, Leofric promised to drop all the taxes except those on horses if she would ride nude through the crowded marketplace. After she did just that with her hair unbound so that only her legs showed, her husband did repeal the taxes.

Later accounts modify the story in that the townspeople were ordered to stay inside with their windows shut. A peeking citizen named **Peeping Tom**, who has sort of become the original patron saint of voyeurs, was subsequently either killed or blinded.

In his poem *Godiva* (1842), Lord **Alfred Tennyson** describes the incident as a supernatural event: "one low churl...peep'd — but his eyes, before they had their will, were shrivll'd into darkness in his head...So the Powers, who wait on noble deeds, cancell'd a sense misused."

While there are skeptics who doubt that Lady Godiva even ever visited Coventry, it is a known fact that she and her husband started and funded a monastery there. Furthermore, it has been proven that two centuries later, during the reign of **Edward** I (1239-1307), only horses in Coventry were being taxed.

**Lady Godiva.**

A medieval knight who never lost a battle, **Rodrigo Dìaz de Vivar** was so renowned for his military skill that during his lifetime he earned the titles **El Cid**, meaning "the lord," and **El Campeador**, meaning "the champion." Today he is admired as a brave and romantic symbol of Spanish national character.

El Cid lived during the beginning of the **Christian** *Reconquista* against **Muslim** rule over Spain. During the rule of **Ferdinand I of Castile**, El Cid ensured his high status by helping to conquer the Moorish kingdom of Sargossa. After Ferdinand's death, El Cid was caught up in the power struggles between Ferdinand's three sons, **Sancho**, **Alfonso** and **Garcia**.

At first, El Cid was the commander or *armiger regis* of Sancho's troops and helped him defeat Garcia and depose and exile Alfonso. But after the childless Sancho died in 1072, Alfonso regained power. Alfonso attempted to win El Cid's loyalty by allowing him to marry his royal niece **Jimena**, but El Cid was no doubt insulted to lose his commander post to **García Ordóñez**, an eminent magnate of the time. El Cid subsequently captured Ordóñez, but it was an unauthorized raid into the Moorish kingdom of Toledo, which was under Alfonso's protection, that led to El Cid's banishment from Castile.

After conquering the Moors several other times, El Cid and Alfonso reconciled. The knight then conquered Valencia and became its independent ruler until his death, although formally he held the land for Alfonso. According to his most illustrious legend, El Cid's last request was that his body be embalmed and seated on his horse during the next battle. When Valencia was attacked by the Moors and the Spanish were near defeat,

**El Cid.**

El Cid's requested appearance either scared away the Moors or else gave the Spanish the inspiration to defeat their attackers.

El Cid's marvelous exploits inspired numerous Spanish poems, romances and plays. The anonymous *Poema de Mio Cid* (c. 1140) portrayed him as temperate and sophisticated, and is also the earliest existing Spanish epic. Later chronicles, starting with the fourteenth or fifteenth century work *Cantar de Rodrigo*, depict him as an immature and impetuous show-off. Famous French spectacles about him include the play *Le Cid* (1637) by **Pierre Corneille** and the 1885 opera of the same name by **Jules Massenet**. He also affected the works of the German philosopher and poet **Johann Gottfried von Herder**, the English poet laureate **Robert Southey**, and the French poet, novelist and dramatist **Victor Hugo**.

Their tragic love affair ranks amongst the fictional ones of **Romeo** and **Juliet** or **Tristan** and **Iseult** (**Isolde**). Details of their affair are known thanks to **Abelard**'s auto-biography, *Historia Calamitatum Mearum* (*History of My Troubles*, c. 1134).

Abelard's brilliant career as one of the Middle Ages' leading rhetoricians and the-ologians reached its climax when he was granted an honorary canonship and the chair of philosophy and theology at the **Notre Dame Cathedral School** in Paris. The students who flocked there to learn from his celebrated mind and earnest man-ner included future bishops and cardinals and even the eventual Pope **Celestine II**.

It was then that Abelard persuaded Canon **Fulbert**, an official at the Cathedral of Notre Dame, to hire him as a live-in tutor for the canon's bright, ravishing niece **Héloïse**. The two virgins began an illicit love affair that was cut short by the horrified canon, who banished Abelard from the house.

When Héloïse learned she was pregnant, Abelard took her to stay in Brittany with his rel-atives, who would raise the lovers' son, **Astralabe**. Abelard then returned to Paris and obtained the canon's forgive-ness on the condi-tion that Héloïse and Abelard marry.

After the wed-ding, Abelard sent Héloïse to the con-vent at Argenteuil, apparently so she could escape her uncle's wrath. In revenge, Fulbert hired some men to break into Abelard's house and castrate him. Abelard completely accepted this as a just punishment, and at his instigation, husband and wife took the vows of the cloth.

When the convent of Argenteuil was dis-persed, Abelard gave Héloïse and her sisters the community he founded at the Paraclete (*le Paraclet*). During this time, the two exchanged several letters.

Héloïse, now an abbess, wrote of her guilt over Abelard's suffering and the fact that she still loved him more than God. While acknowledging their special love, Abelard urged that their love should be devoted to the greater service of God.

Abelard's later writings inspired much controversy and he was condemned by Pope **Innocent II** shortly before his death. The lovers were buried beside each other at the Paraclete, but their remains were later moved to the Père-Lachaise cemetery in Paris.

**Pierre Abelard and Héloïse**

# 15. ROBIN HOOD
## Twelfth century

This celebrated outlaw is commonly characterized as a medieval English individualist who stole from the rich and gave to the poor. The rich are defined, according to the legend, as those who profited from injustice, namely, the **Sheriff of Nottingham** and the abbots of wealthy monasteries. The poor also included women, as his admiration for the **Virgin Mary** was so great that he would aid anyone of her gender — notably the **Maid Marian**, with whom he is romantically linked. **Robin Hood** led a band of like-minded outlaws, whose most prominent members were **Little John**, **Will Scathlok** (or **Scadlok**, or **Scarlet**) and **Much**.

His tales were probably first sung by minstrels (see no. 16) to the yeoman class, who were hard-working farmers or subordinates in royal households. In the twelfth, thirteenth and fourteenth centuries, the dissatisfied lower classes frequently rebelled against the monied barons, climaxing in the **Peasants' Revolt of 1381**. Robin Hood, an able fighter and free-spirited dweller of Nottinghamshire's **Sherwood Forest**, was the hero of these malcontents.

That Robin Hood ever lived has been a hotly-contested debate among historians, some of whom have suggested that he was a disinherited follower of the soldier and statesman **Simon de Montfort** (c. 1208-1265) or that he lived during the reigns of **Richard I** (1157-1199) or **Edward IV** (1422-1483).

In the fourteenth or early fifteenth century, 38 of these ballads were recorded, but it is the post-medieval ones that are the best known. In one early ballad, *"A Gest of Robin Hood,"* he lends a large sum of money to a poor knight who is in debt to a greedy abbot. Robin Hood's collateral is a vow to the Virgin Mary. Later, after stealing twice the amount from the abbot's monastery, Robin Hood refused the knight's money, saying the Virgin Mary already took care of it.

During the sixteenth century, the idea that Robin Hood was a fallen noble originated, as well as the addition to the legend of Maid Marian. Since that time, Robin Hood has been the protagonist of at least 60 pieces of prose, 30 plays, and several operas and motion pictures, in which he has been portrayed by **Douglas Fairbanks**, **Errol Flynn**, **Peter Ustinov** and **Kevin Costner**. He also appears as a character in Sir **Walter Scott**'s *Ivanhoe* (1820) and **T.H. White**'s *The Once and Future King* (1958).

**Robin Hood.**

While he lived, this king was a skilled politician, an extraordinary soldier and a talented lyric poet. Later he would become perceived as the typical fierce and courageous warrior of the Middle Ages.

**Richard I** was the third son of **Henry II** and **Eleanor of Aquitaine**. Various power struggles within his family caused him to unite with **Philip II Augustus** of France (1165-1223) to wage war against his father, who died two days after acknowledging Richard's right to the throne.

After receiving Normandy from Philip and being crowned king of England at Westminster in 1189, Richard began planning the **Third Crusade** to the **Holy Land** to recapture Jerusalem from the **Muslims**. He sold many of England's possessions and increased taxes to raise a formidable army and fleet. Richard conquered the Italian seaport of Messina as well as Cyprus before joining the other Crusaders at Acre in 1191.

Notwithstanding Richard's hot-headed quarrels with Philip II and **Leopold V**, the duke of Austria, Acre was taken by the Crusaders. Richard captured Joppa (now Jaffa, near Tel Aviv) in a glorious victory, but despite two attempts, the Crusaders failed to capture Jerusalem. However, Richard negotiated a three-year truce that allowed the Crusaders to hold Acre and gave Christians access to the holy places.

Sailing home, Richard was shipwrecked and taken prisoner by Leopold V, who gave Richard to **Henry VI** of the Holy Roman Empire. Meanwhile, the English had no idea where their king was.

During his imprisonment, Richard's famous chance meeting supposedly occurred with his favorite minstrel, the French **Blondel de Nefle**. In medieval England, minstrels sang or recited stories accompanied by musical instruments. After each sang half of a song that they had written together, Blondel told the English where Richard was being held. Regardless, Richard was forced to pay a steep ransom to win his freedom.

He briefly returned to England to be recrowned and set out to save Normandy. After a five-year war, peace was made in 1199. Richard died that same year during a siege on the castle of the **Vicompte of Limoges**, who refused to give the king some gold a peasant had discovered.

**Richard the Lion-hearted.**

# ROBERT BRUCE
## 1274-1329

This king who rescued Scotland from English rule is today venerated as a Scottish national hero. Born to a noble family that was related to the deposed Scottish royal family, until his early 30s, **Robert I** was outwardly loyal to the English king **Edward I** (1239-1307), even helping to defeat the rebel **William Wallace** (c. 1272-1305).

Then, perhaps sensing that it was possible to win Scottish independence, he began gathering followers. He or his minions then killed **John Comyn**, who was a possible rival for the throne. After being crowned in March of 1306, Robert had to defend his country against Edward I, who regarded Robert as another rebellious traitor.

Two crushing defeats led to the capture of Robert's wife and many supporters as well as the execution of three of his brothers. Robert went into hiding on a remote island. A legend says that during this low period he gained optimism and patience from watching a spider diligently weaving its web.

After Edward I died, Robert began a fresh campaign against **Edward II** (1284-1327). He recovered most of Scotland, goading Edward II into an invasion of the country. Although the British forces were three times the size of Robert's, he defeated the English at the 1314 **Battle of Bannockburn**, regarded as Robert's greatest achievement.

**Robert Bruce.**

Robert then raided England several times, once almost capturing Edward II. In 1323, the pope recognized Robert as the king of Scotland, and in 1328 the English, under **Edward III** (1312-1377), accepted Scottish independence in the **Treaty of Northampton**.

Robert died the following year, possibly of leprosy. At his request, Robert's heart was removed to be taken to the **Holy Land** by Sir **James Douglas**, who was killed on the way. One legend says the heart was found and taken to the now-ruined **Melrose Abbey** in southeast Scotland.

Like so many fabled heroes, it is disputed whether **William Tell** ever existed. While his legend records him as a courageous peasant leader in the Swiss struggle for freedom from Austria, William Tell has come to signify political and individual freedom to people all over the world.

Tell's adventures began when a tyrannical Austrian bailiff named **Gessler** ordered the citizens of Uri to acknowledge Austrian domination by paying homage to a cap hung in a public square. Tell, a leader of the rebellious Swiss, refused, and was forced to shoot an apple from the head of his son. This dramatic scene has been reproduced countless times by artists in every visual form, from paintings and etchings to cartoons and films.

After succeeding, William Tell was taken prisoner on a boat because he had threatened Gessler. A violent storm prevented the boat from landing, and because of his strength and skill, Tell was permitted to take the rudder. After landing the boat, he escaped and subsequently killed Gessler in an ambush. Tell is said to have later fought at the **Battle of Morganten** in 1315 and died in a flood in 1350.

Tell's exploits first appeared in fifteenth century ballads and were then chronicled in various historical texts. *Guillaume Tell* (1791), an opera by **André Grétry**, found a rapt audience in Paris, then in the throes of the **French Revolution**. The tale was next retold by the dramatist **J.C. Friedrich von Schiller** in the play *Wilhelm Tell* (1804). However, it is the riveting overture of **Gioacchino Antonio Rossini**'s opera *Guillaume Tell* (1829) that has proven to be the most enduring tribute to the brave patriot.

William Tell.

# HIAWATHA
## Fifteenth century

Until 1855, this marvelous legend was confined mostly to the members of the six tribes of **Hiawatha**'s native **Iroquois**. In their lore, Hiawatha enjoys a larger-than-life status as someone who saved his people from violent discord, a similar reputation to the one King **Arthur** (see no. 9) had in the centuries following his death. However, unlike King Arthur, Hiawatha never fought anyone. Rather, he simply established a lasting and orderly peace.

Hiawatha's Native American name was **Ojibwa**, meaning "he who makes rivers," and he was chief of the **Onandaga tribe** of the Iroquois. Before Hiawatha's feats, upper New York State was the site of constant warfare among the tribes that resided there.

In about 1450, Hiawatha managed to ally these tribes — Cayuga, Mohawk, Oneida, Onandaga and Seneca — into the **Five Nations of the Iroquois**, also called the Iroquois League. Thanks to his able planning skills, each unit of the confederacy still retained its independence.

After his death, the Iroquois elevated Hiawatha to a cultural hero, viewing him as a magical prophet and the earthly embodiment of progress and civilization. In their mythology, his actions come at the direct request of the oracle **Dekanawidah**. His people also credit Hiawatha with teaching them farming, healing, navigation and art techniques, all the while working with the forces of nature.

Hiawatha's widespread notoriety would not come until **Henry Wadsworth Longfellow**, deliberately trying to create an American tradition, published his *Song of Hiawatha* (1855). It has 22 sections, including ones on his childhood, his fasting, his friends, his sailing, his fishing and his wedding day. Longfellow describes Hiawatha as having many superhuman skills, like the ability to "shoot an arrow from him/And run forward with such fleetness/That the arrow fell behind him!"

Written in the meter of the Finnish epic *Kalevala*, the poem's fame was guaranteed by the immediate controversy it raised over its plagiarism and shaky basis in actual fact. All this attention led to the highest sales a poem had ever received. Public readings and parodies followed in its wake, and today the poem that made Hiawatha a household name is regarded as one of Longfellow's best.

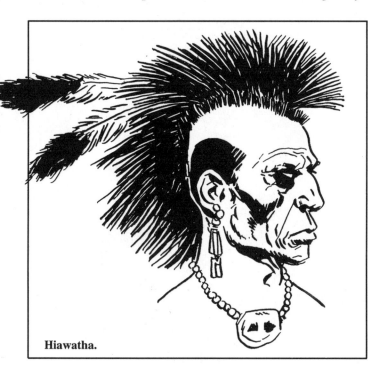

Hiawatha.

# JOAN OF ARC (JEANNE d'ARC)
## 1414-1431

This French national heroine and saint of the **Roman Catholic Church** gained her renown during the **Hundred Years' War** with England. Since then, she has been the subject of countless works of art and over 100 plays, the most famous of which are by **J.C. Friedrich von Schiller** (1801) and **George Bernard Shaw** (1923).

**Joan** was an illiterate but pious peasant girl who began having religious visions and hearing the voices of saints at age 13. When she was 17, these voices convinced her that her calling was to restore national unity to France by driving the English away and seeing that the dauphin (the eldest son of a king) **Charles** (1403-1461) was crowned king at Reims, where all French kings were crowned. Although in southern France

**Joan of Arc.**

Charles was recognized as ruler, the English and the Burgundians (French citizens in favor of the British) controlled Paris and northern France, where Reims was located.

When Joan appeared in his court with her strange story, Charles, although broke and desperate, tested her. He let a noble sit on his throne, but Joan saw through the deception. After Joan told him what he asked from God when he prayed alone, Charles gave her a suit of armor and some troops and sent her to the besieged Orleans.

Once she got there, Joan led a series of skillful assaults that made the British flee in about a week. The English were so fearstruck by her presence that an English proclamation was issued against those that deserted their cause "for fear of the mayde." While she was wounded several times, Joan later claimed to have killed no one.

After recovering several occupied towns on the way to Reims, Joan stood by

during the 1429 coronation of King **Charles VII**. While trying to recapture Paris, she was taken prisoner by the Burgundians, who delivered her to the English for 16,000 francs. After an unfair trial in Rouen in which she was pronounced a heretic (a religious disbeliever), Joan was burned at the stake before a huge crowd. Her courageous behavior there made many of them fear that they'd just seen a saint martyred.

In 1445, her **Trial of Rehabilitation** proclaimed her sentence void, and a statue of her was erected on the site on which she had died. She was declared a saint by Pope **Benedict XV** in 1920, and the day of her death, May 30th, became her feast day. One of the most interesting legends about Joan of Arc is that another person was substituted for her at the execution and that the real Joan appeared in her native village several years later.

# 21. VLAD THE IMPALER (VLAD DRACUL) 1431-1477

After hearing tales of **Vlad the Impaler** and Romanian **vampires**, English author **Bram Stoker** had the nightmare about a vampire king rising from his tomb that inspired his book *Dracula* (1897). Regarded as one of the greatest horror novels ever written, it has served as inspiration for numerous "Dracula" movies, from **Tod Browning**'s 1931 classic with **Bela Lugosi** in the title role, to **Francis Ford Coppola**'s 1993 remake starring **Gary Oldman**.

These films, and other monster movies loosely based on the grisly legend, have assured this cruel king of Wallachia (now Romania) a grisly immortality. While the fictional Count Dracula (which means "son of the devil") of Transylvania is known for attacking in order to drink blood, the real Dracula was far more dangerous, as he is estimated to have killed over 100,000 people during his six-year reign.

At about the age of 12, Dracula was made a hostage of the Turks by his father, **Vlad II**, in a sort of diplomatic measure. He was released after his father's death, and after one failed attempt, Vlad seized the Wallachian throne in 1456 and began his tyrannical regime. His "thin and reddish face in which the large, wide-open green eyes were framed by bushy black eyebrows" was described as threatening, and his merciless control became so absolute that crime amongst the terrorized Wallachians was practically nonexistent.

Vlad's favorite method of execution was a slow, painful death by impalement, in which a greased stake was inserted into the victim's private parts or stomach so that the point eventually came out of the throat or mouth. These impalements were used as

**Vlad the Impaler.**

entertainment during meals, and once, when a sickened guest held his nose, he was impaled too.

Vlad was disturbed by the homeless population, so he invited all its members to a banquet in a large dining hall. He entered and asked if they would like to be without any cares. They shouted their assent, so he had the building boarded up and set on fire.

After initiating several Transylvanian attacks in which villages were literally removed from maps, Vlad went to war against the Turks in 1461. While appealing to King **Mathias** of Hungary for aid, Dracula was taken prisoner. For amusement during his 12-year imprisonment, he tortured small animals in his cell. Eventually released, he retook the throne in 1476. But his army was soon ambushed by Turks and Vlad was killed in battle, possibly by his own troops.

This fallen emperor is a tragic and sympathetic figure, a symbol of the great Aztec civilization's dramatic demise at the hands of Spanish conquerors. However, if **Montezuma** had never encountered the notorious **Hernán Cortéz** (1485-1547), he would never have later become the prototypical Aztec.

Montezuma became the namesake of a group of pre-Columbian **Pueblo Indian** cliff dwellings because the settlers who came across them erroneously surmised them to be of Aztec origin. His name has even become a slang expression, Montezuma's revenge, which refers to the diarrhea vacationers get in Mexico from differences in water content.

In about 1502, Montezuma succeeded his uncle **Ahuitzotl** as the autocrat of an empire that stretched from Mexico to today's Honduras and Nicaragua. Montezuma waged constant wars to expand his territory and acquire prisoners for religious sacrifices. By 1519, his empire had more than five million inhabitants, many of them exasperated with their ruler's never-ending demands for tributes and sacrificial victims.

The Aztecs believed that in 1519, the white, bearded god **Quetzalcoatl** would return to claim the throne. But instead, the white, bearded Cortéz landed on Mexico's east coast. Once he became aware of this belief, Cortéz used it to his advantage in making alliances with the dissatisfied Aztecs as he travelled through Mexico. Montezuma, clearly intimidated, tried to buy Cortés off with lavish gifts, but it was in vain.

In November of 1519, Montezuma received Cortéz in the capital city of Tenochtitlán (near Mexico City) and was taken captive. Assured of his safety, Cortés ruled for several months. During this time, Montezuma's capitulation diminished his reputation among his remaining supporters.

In June, after the Spaniards violently stopped a religious festival, the citizens of Tenochtitlán revolted. Montezuma attempted to appease them, but was assailed with stones and arrows. Montezuma died three days later, from either the wounds he sustained or at the hands of the Spaniards.

Believing that Cortéz had murdered their ruler, the Aztecs nearly annihilated the Spanish forces when they tried to creep out of the city at night. Under the subsequent rulers **Cuitláhuac** and **Cuahtémoc**, the Aztecs fought off the Spaniards until August of 1521, when Cortéz' troops invaded and destroyed Tenochtitlán.

Montezuma II.

This Renaissance political thinker and historian is best-known for his idea of a political morality that is based on power and completely separate from traditional ethical norms. His maxims, such as "To be feared gives more security that to be loved" and "A prudent ruler cannot and should not observe faith when such observance is to his disadvantage," have drawn shock and debate since he wrote them. His philosophy is widely regarded as the decisive break between political thought in the Middle Ages and modern times.

Born to a poor but prominent Florentine family, **Niccolò Machiavelli** is believed to have been mostly self-taught. When he was 25, **Charles VIII** of France invaded Italy, commencing a tangled conflict that would eventually involve all of Western and Central Europe. Once an independent hub of Italian politics, Florence became enmeshed in the rivalry between the emperor, the pope and the French king, creating an atmosphere that welcomed searches for rational explanations.

Starting in 1498, Machiavelli served in the chancellery of the Florentine republic. There he was second in command as well as the secretary of the **Ten of Basilia**, a committee in charge of diplomatic negotiations and military supervision. His travels within Italy and to France and Germany gave him the working background for his writings.

When the Medici regained power in 1512, he was dismissed and subsequently imprisoned, accused of participating in a conspiracy against the new rulers. Even though he was tortured, he never confessed.

Once released, he was forbidden to enter Florence for a year. Machiavelli considered this involuntary retirement to be the greatest tragedy of his life, but through it he became a political writer. Although restored to favor by the pope in 1525-1526, Machiavelli died the following year.

Machiavelli's views have been accepted or rejected in varying degrees throughout the ensuing centuries. His most famous work, *The Prince* (1513), is viewed as a handbook for tyrants, emphasizing the importance of willpower and the internal conflict between fortune and virtue. His philosophy was vehemently attacked in the sixteenth and seventeenth centuries, but by the eighteenth century, it began to gain wider acceptance. More recently, the rise of totalitarianism has given his work a new relevance.

**Niccolò Machiavelli**

**Leonardo da Vinci**'s most famous portrait, *The Mona Lisa* (or *La Giaconda*), has become one of Western civilization's most widely-reproduced images, making it as familiar as the **Eiffel Tower** or the **Golden Gate Bridge**. The reason for *The Mona Lisa*'s fame is not simply because of its artistic significance, but rather due to its subject's enigmatic, close-lipped smile.

The explanation behind this shadow of a grin has been at the center of an endless debate that can never be decisively solved. Theories include that she was mourning the death of her baby girl, that she was considering whether or not to take a lover, or that she was in pain after having a tooth pulled. The most extreme hypothesis suggests that while she may have lived, the painting's subject was the deceptive Leonardo himself, which would explain why he would choose to paint someone whose looks were considered to be quite plain.

However, it is generally acknowledged that **Lisa Giaconda** was indeed the subject. Born in Naples to a poor family, at age 16 **Lisa di Anton** became the third wife of **Francesco Giaconda**, a Florentine merchant who was 19 years her senior. In 1503, Giaconda commissioned Leonardo to paint a portrait of his 24-year-old wife for his dining room wall.

By 1507, Giaconda's impatience led him to terminate the sittings and refuse to pay for the unfinished portrait. Later that same year, Mona (short for Madonna) Lisa left Florence with her husband on a business trip to Calabria, and there her concrete records in the pages of history end. In 1509, her name was removed from the tax rolls of Florence and she vanished into obscurity. Perhaps she died. Perhaps she went on to lead a long life in a different city. No one knows.

If more details of her life were known, Mona Lisa would probably not be consid-

**Lisa Giaconda,** *The Mona Lisa.*

ered so mysterious and even mythical today. It is this quality of hers that inspired an unforgettable song made popular by **Nat King Cole**.

Fortunately, Leonardo was unaffected by Giaconda's rejection and took the painting with him to Paris. The painting's relaxed subject and stirring juxtaposition, with the foreground's serene face contrasted by the background's precipitous rocks and meandering rivers, established a new standard of **High Renaissance** portraiture.

*The Mona Lisa* was eventually hung in the **Louvre** after being sold to King **Francis I** (1494-1547), supposedly for the current equivalent of $50,000. In 1911, the priceless painting was stolen. Before it was recovered two years later, six Americans paid $300,000 apiece for forgeries.

This enigmatic seer's reputation grows every time one of his cryptically worded predictions seems to come to pass. What truly distinguished **Nostradamus** is that he recorded the actual names of people who would later change the world, including **Napoleon**, **Pasteur** and **Hitler**. Though his predictions read like riddles laced with obscure symbolism, Nostradamus also seems to have accurately foreseen major historical events, such as the great London fire of 1666, the founding of America and the fall of the Berlin Wall.

**Nostradamus**

After the sudden deaths of his wife and sons, Nostradamus closed his medical practice in Agen, France and wandered throughout Europe for a decade. During this time, Nostradamus is said to have seen a young Franciscan friar in Italy and bowed at his feet, saying "I must kneel before His Holiness." Nineteen years after the psychic's death, the same friar became Pope **Sixtus V**.

In 1544, Nostradamus settled in Salon, France, to practice medicine and astrology. The visions he had after staring for hours into a water-filled brass bowl mounted on a tripod were recorded in his book of 11 rhymed verses, *Centuries* (1555). Nostradamus used abundant puns, anagrams and scientific jargon to blur the content.

Of Hitler, Nostradamus predicted his name as "Hister," and wrote of his misleading ideology and mysterious death.

Nostradamus also seemed to know of Napoleon's exile, escape, defeat at Waterloo and desolate death. After these two tyrants, Nostradamus also predicts the defeat of a "third **Antichrist**" and his "foreign Arabian" followers, as well as a period of "Plague, Famine, Death by military hand" slated to begin in late 1999.

His first prediction to come true was the 1559 accidental death of **Henry II** of France. Nostradamus wrote: "In martial field by a single duel/In a golden cage he shall put out his eye/Two wounds from one, then he shall die a cruel death." During a friendly joust, Henry was wounded simultaneously in the eye and throat when his opponent's lance penetrated the golden visor of the king's helmet.

Due to his startling accuracy, Henry's widow **Catherine de Médici** invited Nostradamus to the royal court at Paris to be her adviser, and possibly her lover as well. Other leaders combed his book for hints of what was to come, and Nostradamus soon became known as the greatest **Renaissance** seer.

Eventually returning to Salon due to failing health, Nostradamus foresaw his own death and secretly arranged to have a metal plaque buried with him. The plaque remained undiscovered until 1700, when his grave was opened. The plaque read: "1700."

# 26. ANNE BOLEYN
## 1507-1536

Her well-known historical role as one of King **Henry VIII**'s beheaded wives has rendered her an unforgettably tragic figure. Feminists decry her unjust demise as evidence of patriarchy at its worst. Yet it is the horrid fate of this queen that has produced eerie legends about her vengeful ghost and the fate of her remains.

**Anne Boleyn** was only 15 when she moved from Paris into Henry VIII's court, where she soon gained many admirers. The king's first wife and mother of **Mary I** of England, **Catherine of Aragon**, was already in her late 30s. While Henry probably initially cared for Anne, it was his urgent desire for a male heir that dictated most of his actions.

When Anne was going to marry a lord, Henry got a cardinal to prevent it. However, to marry Anne, Henry was forced to break ties with the **Roman Catholic Church**, bringing about the **English Reformation**. Henry and Anne were secretly married in January of 1533, later announcing it on Easter. In late May, on Henry's orders, the **Archbishop of Canterbury** pronounced the king's first marriage void.

More than her arrogant behavior at court and Henry's wandering eye, it was the birth of her daughter, the future Queen **Elizabeth I**, that put Anne in jeopardy. Anne's fate was sealed by a 1534 miscarriage and a 1536 birth of a stillborn son.

In early May, Henry had Anne imprisoned in the **Tower of London** on charges of adultery and incest. Had she not been convicted, the king planned to try her as a witch. She was executed on May 19th, and Henry remarried 11 days later.

It is said that before her burial, Anne's heart was stolen and secretly hidden in a church near Thetford in Suffolk. It was discovered three centuries after her death and reburied under the church's organ. There is also a belief that her body was removed from its official resting place at the chapel of **St. Peter-ad-Vincula** and laid under an unmarked black marble slab.

Anne Boleyn's most fabulous legacy, however, is her supposed ghost, which is reputed to haunt the Tower of London and the chapel at St. Peter-ad-Vincula. Tradition holds that every year, on May 19th, Anne, her head on her knees, sits in a coach driven by a headless attendant and drawn by four headless horses. This procession slowly travels through Norfolk and vanishes at the front door of her childhood home, Blicking Hall.

**Anne Boleyn**

# GUY FAWKES
## 1570-1606

A fervent **Catholic** who was part unsuccessful revolutionary and part involuntary martyr, **Guy Fawkes** lived in a time when the members of his religion were subject to many oppressive laws enacted by the ruling **Protestants**. His role as the best remembered participant in the audacious **Gunpowder Plot**, an ill-fated plan to blow up London's **Parliament** building, is celebrated every year in England on November 5th as **Guy Fawkes Day**. The festivities involve fireworks, masked children requesting "a penny for the guy," and numerous burnings of miniature Fawkes effigies.

Born to a prominent Yorkshire family, Fawkes was raised a Protestant but converted after his mother married a Catholic. At age 23, Fawkes, a handsome man with a full auburn beard, sold his many land holdings and left England to fight for the Spanish army, where he quickly distinguished himself as a courageous soldier.

However, it was Fawkes' religious enthusiasm, his unknown face and his military knowledge that brought him to the attention of the fanatical Gunpowder plotters. They sent a messenger to enlist Fawkes, and in 1604 he returned to England.

Using an alias and posing as a servant, Fawkes rented a house close to the Parliament. From it, the group began tunneling under the government structure. Two months later, they discovered a passageway into the building's basement. There they placed iron bars and rocks over 36 barrels of gunpowder so that the explosion would be sure to kill everyone inside, including King **James I** (1556-1625) and the Protestant members of Parliament.

Then, as British history was about to be unequivocally altered, one of the conspirators, **William Parker**, reverted to Protestantism and reported the plot, winning himself a pension of £700 a year.

On November 4th, just as he was about to ignite the gunpowder, Fawkes was arrested. Taken to the **Tower of London**, Fawkes initially refused to answer any questions. But after torture on the rack, he signed a full confession that provided his real name and those of the other plotters.

Convicted of treason, Fawkes remained brave until the bitter end, refusing to denounce Catholicism. On January 31, Fawkes and seven other conspirators were hanged, beheaded and drawn and quartered opposite the building they'd tried so hard to destroy.

**Guy Fawkes.**

This **Native American**, whose name means "playful," became a folk hero because she twice temporarily halted enmities between her people and the **English settlers** who colonized Virginia.

The daughter of **Wahusonacook** (aka **Powhatan**, 1550-1618), who ruled a loose alliance of **Algonquin** people in tidewater Virginia, **Pocahontas** was also called **Matoaka**. In 1607, English colonists founded Jamestown on her tribe's land, and several hostile incidents ensued. Nevertheless, young Pocahontas visited the settlement and became acquainted with its residents.

According to Captain **James Smith**'s *Generalle Historie* (1624), the adventurer was ambushed and taken captive by the Native Americans in 1607. Pocahontas pleaded with her father in vain, but Smith's head was forcefully placed upon a sacrificial stone. She successfully stopped the ritual when she "took my head in her arms and laid her own upon it to save me from death."

The incident led to a precarious truce that was weakened by Smith's 1609 return to England. After the aggressive Sir **Thomas Dale** was made the acting governor, Wahusonacook moved his people further inland.

Pocahontas was taken prisoner by deception when she was about 18, although during her captivity she was treated graciously. In 1614, she converted to **Christianity** and was baptized as **Rebecca**. That April, she married Lord **John Rolfe**, an esteemed colonist who was one of the first cultivators of tobacco. This union enabled Dale and Wahusonacook to negotiate a truce that would last until 1622.

In the captivating and pretty princess, now Lady Rebecca Rolfe, Dale saw the possibility of additional funds for the Lon-

**Pocahontas.**

don Company of Virginia. So in 1616, the governor took the Rolfes and their infant son **Thomas** to England. There, Pocahontas was presented at court and treated as a celebrity. She also had a touching reunion with Smith.

As her family was about to return to North America, Pocahontas contracted smallpox and died. Her remains stayed in England, where they were buried by the altar of **St. George's Church** in Gravesend.

In 1995, **Disney** released an enchanting animated account of Pocahontas' life. It is the first full-length animated feature that the company devoted to a historical figure.

# JOHN and PRISCILLA ALDEN
## Seventeenth century

Although he is an important historical figure due to his prominent role in America's colonial times, **John Alden** owes his romantic status to his descendant, **Henry Wadsworth Longfellow**, who also immortalized **Hiawatha** (see no. 19).

Born in England in 1599, Alden was a cooper (a barrelmaker) for the London merchants who financed the 1620 *Mayflower* expedition in which a group of religious outcasts from England endured immense hardship to found a North American colony, and ultimately to become the founding parents of New England society. A founder of the English colony of Plymouth in what is now Massachusetts, Alden was supposedly the first to set foot on **Plymouth Rock**.

After possibly failing to win the hand of **Priscilla Mullens** for his friend, the military leader **Miles Standish**, John and Priscilla wed in 1623. Their union would produce 11 children.

In about 1627, Standish and Alden founded the town of Duxbury near Plymouth. There Alden held a number of civic offices, including surveyor of highways, deputy of Duxbury and a member of the local council of war. Alden was also a farmer, and aided Standish in resolving boundary disputes as well as in raising forces for defense against **Native American** attacks.

Alden was later assistant governor of Massachusetts for 44 years. He also served as deputy governor twice and held the position of treasurer for two years. When he died in 1687, he was the last surviving signer of the **Mayflower Compact**.

After the tremendous success of his *Song of Hiawatha*, Longfellow wrote about the first colonists in *The Courtship of Miles Standish* (1858). While its basis in fact is dubious at best, it is an enchanting tale.

John Alden, "fair-haired, azure-eyed, with delicate Saxon complexion," is described secretly pining away for Priscilla, "the loveliest maiden of Plymouth." Standish, "a blunt old Captain" asks his friend to propose to Priscilla for him. After an internal struggle in which "friendship prevailed over love," Alden agrees.

He finds Priscilla and speaks at length of Standish's attributes. In reply, she says, "Why don't you speak for yourself, John?" John tells this to Standish, who gets angry. When Priscilla and John hear a false rumor that Standish perished in a Native American scuffle, they decide to marry. On their wedding day, the penitent Standish appears and gives the couple his blessing.

**John Alden and Priscilla Mullens.**

# 30. ANTONIO STRADIVARI
## 1644-1737

The acoustically perfect violins of **Antonio Stradivari** are the Rolls-Royces of their kind, unparalleled to this day and also mysterious, as it is still not known exactly what makes them so faultless. His single-minded and lifelong devotion to his ingenious work also brought about the redesigns of several instruments.

All this resulted in Stradivari's perception as almost divine by his Italian countrymen and all types of musicians and artisans. This worship spread to popular culture, so that his Latin name, **Stradivarius**, is today instantly equated with the greatest and most priceless violins ever made.

After an apprenticeship with the violin maker **Niccolò Amati**, Stradivarius began making his own models in 1666. At first his work was similar to the smaller, thickly yellow-varnished models of his teacher, but in 1684 Stradivarius began modifying this form. In these larger models, which have a deeper-colored varnish, the great master began experimenting with variations in the instrument's minute and then-established traditional details.

By the first years of the eighteenth century, Stradivarius had completely innovated the violin's proportions. His improvements mostly involved making the body more shallow, issuing a stronger and more permeating tone. It is his varnish that many consider to be his instruments' really distinguishing feature, and its precise recipe has not yet been determined.

During his life, Stradivarius would similarly revise the forms of the viola and the cello. However, it is **violins** for which he is famed, with the 1715 *Alard* thought to be the ultimate culmination of Stradivarius' expertise and skill. He is believed to have created about 1,000 other instruments, but only half of these still exist.

Stradivarius taught and was assisted by his sons, **Francisco** and **Omobono**. While Stradivarius' early instruments have a label with a Maltese Cross and the initials "A.S.," ensuing ones have his sons' initials as well. In an attempt to increase the instruments' value, many of these later labels were replaced with phony ones that claimed only the elder Stradivari's workmanship.

**Antonio Stradivari**

While they plagued the seas, **pirates** were feared as ruthless and sadistic predators, but due to **Hollywood**, these same pirates are today glorified as adventurous and romantic rebels. Next to the fictional Captain Hook and **Robert Louis Stevenson**'s Long John Silver, Captain **William Kidd** is one of the most celebrated pirates, thanks to the legend of his still-unfound buried treasure that has baited fortune hunters on searches from Nova Scotia to the South China Sea.

This Scottish-born minister's son began his career as a **privateer** (a ship captain hired by a government to attack enemy ships) for England in the West Indies. After moving to America, Kidd was commissioned as a privateer against any French vessels or pirates harassing English ships. Kidd's payment was to be whatever he could take from these enemies.

In November 1696, Kidd and his crew sailed for the Indian Ocean on the *Adventure Galley*. After a year of futile searching, Kidd became a pirate when, in the Red Sea, he began storming every ship he came across, including those he was supposed to protect. During a mutiny, Kidd killed his gunner, and much of his crew subsequently deserted him in Madagascar. When his ship reached the West Indies, Kidd learned he had been declared a pirate.

Travelling back to America to protest his innocence, Kidd arrived in New York in 1698. There he stored some of his treasure with the **Gardiner family**, who owned an island in Long Island Sound. Their descendants today maintain that the captain's ghost still wanders the family mansion at night, and that they still have remnants of one of Kidd's gifts, a gold cloth.

Kidd subsequently sailed to Boston, where he was arrested. Sent to England's **Old Bailey** for a trial, Kidd's claims that his crew had forced him into piracy were not

**Captain William Kidd.**

allowed into evidence. Found guilty of piracy, Kidd was hanged on May 23, 1701.

While authorities seized what they could find of Kidd's booty, they did not believe they recovered all of it. This prompted the pirate's immediate and international renown, as well as the numerous tales about his mythical cache.

More than a century later, **Edgar Allen Poe** is said to have believed that Kidd secretly buried the bulk of his treasure on the Gardiner's island with a cryptogram map of numbers to remind him of its site. According to this story, after searching for it fruitlessly, he used the experience for *The Gold Bug* (1843). Still another common belief is that his treasure lies on the barren Screecham's Island, located off the coast of Cape Cod, where it is guarded eternally by ghosts.

The rhymes of **Mother Goose** that have charmed children for so long come from a large European mass of satirical ballads and folk songs. They are believed to recount various royal love scandals as well as the political and religious struggles of their day. As records of their time that were first transmitted orally, the verses are direct descendants of **Homer**'s epics (see no. 3).

The real mystery of Mother Goose, however, is who she was, if she was actually a person and not a handy label to affix to a large bed of folklore. Speculations include that this eternal teller of tales was the biblical **Queen of Sheba**. Another theory is that she was **Charlemagne**'s mother, Queen **Bertha** or **Reine Pedance**, who died in 783 and was nicknamed "Queen Goose-foot" or "Goose-Footed Bertha." It has even been suggested that the

**Elizabeth Vergoose.**

great **William Shakespeare** (1564-1616) wrote some of the rhymes.

Americans also have their own traditional Mother Goose in the person of **Elizabeth Vergoose**. Apparently during her life this colonial Bostonite became locally associated with the folklore figure, especially by youngsters. She used the songs and rhymes she remembered from her youth to entertain her widowed husbands' 16 children and her grandchildren.

Her son-in-law, **Thomas Fleet**, is said to have collected and published these as *Songs for the Nursery*, or *Mother Goose's Melodies* (1719). However, no copy of this book has been found.

That Fleet's book was the first of its kind is dispelled by the concrete existence of a French book called *Histoires ou Contes du Temps Passé avec des Moralités* (*Histories or Tales of Long Ago with Morals*, 1697). On the cover, a woman sits at a spinning wheel, telling tales to a man, a boy, a girl and a cat. A sign on the wall reads "Contes de Ma Mère L'Oye" ("Tales of Mother Goose").

Mother Goose is usually drawn as an old woman with a distinctively crooked noise and a pointed chin. She is either illustrated flying through the air on the back of a goose with a tall hat and a magic wand, or else in a domestic setting with children clustered around her.

The rhyme "Sing a song of sixpence" is believed to document King **Henry VIII**'s ubiquitous greed and his attraction to **Anne Boleyn** (see no. 26). The first line refers to Henry's humming over seized abbey revenues. Meanwhile, Queen Catherine of Aragon eats the "bread" of England. Not a servant but rather a maiden, Anne is hanging her Parisian gowns out to dry. Her "snipped off" nose refers to Henry's halting of her planned marriage by a clerical "blackbird," as well as Anne's execution.

During the twentieth century, the enchanting tall tales attributed to Baron **Karl Friedrich Hieronymus von Münchhausen** have evolved from their traditional role as bedtime stories to become larger-than-life images on the big screen.

The first such treatment was a German film released in the early 1940s, subsequently dubbed "a rallying cry for the **Third Reich**." A Czech animated feature followed in 1962, but it was a Columbia picture, *The Adventures of Baron Münchausen* (1988), that really propelled the storyteller into the public's mass-media consciousness.

With a budget estimated between $40 and $50 million, the extravaganza starred **John Neville** in the lead, with **Eric Idle** and **Robin Williams** playing supporting roles. In the film, which bears no resemblance to the baron's tales, Münchausen, with the help of a little girl and his superhuman servants, saves Vienna from Turkish troops.

The real baron also fought those troops, but in Russia, serving in the Russian army as an officer in two wars against the Turks between 1737 and 1739. After that, the aristocratic hunter and sportsman retired to his estate in Hanover, where he gained a reputation as an excellent storyteller.

The first collections of stories to use his name was printed in Germany in *Vademecum fur lustige Leute* (1781-1783), although several of these can be traced to earlier sources. Like the name **Mother Goose** (see no.32) was cited as the source of any well-known rhyme, the baron apparently became a suitable personage to attach to a large body of fantastic travelers' tales. A typical anecdote tells of a man tying his horse to a stake during a snowstorm, only to awaken after a night's thaw to find the animal dangling from a high steeple.

The next version was written in English by an exiled German, **Rudolf Erich Raspe**, who may have known the baron. Called *Baron Münchausen's Narrative of His Marvelous Travels and Campaigns in Russia* (1785), the booklet contained preposterous boasts and sold extremely well.

A German translation then appeared, as well as an edition lengthened by other contributors that was called *Gulliver Revived or the Singular Travels, Voyages, and Adventures of Baron Münchausen.* (1786). Later, more tales were fabricated about the baron in other books, including *The Adventures of Baron Münchausen* (1793).

The baron's reputation for deception has even led to an emotional disorder, Münchausen's syndrome, to be named for him. The disease causes patients to invent symptoms to get medical attention, sometimes even making themselves ill to achieve this end.

Baron Münchausen condemned the lies he supposably said, and attempted in vain to dodge the visitors his fame attracted. After being dubbed the world's biggest boaster, he died in grief.

**Baron von Münchhausen**

Like the fictional **Don Juan**, this Italian folk hero's name is used today to describe any womanizer. This reputation comes from his perhaps slightly exaggerated memoirs, in which **Giovanni Giacomo Casanova** portrayed himself as a bold adventurer who completely lacked the moral principles of his time.

Casanova, who once said that women were his cuisine, wrote that he lured thousands of women into his bed, even naming 116 of them. His favorite targets were his friends' wives or daughters, and he frequently seduced two at the same time. Often the consummate bachelor bathed with his lovers in a bathtub built for two, or shared his favorite breakfast of 50 oysters with them.

It is fitting that Casanova was the son of an actor, for throughout his colorful career he worked in a wide variety of trades. After being kicked out of a seminary for unseemly behavior, he became a secretary for a Roman Catholic Cardinal in Rome, but a scandal, the first of many, caused him to leave the city. Casanova then travelled to Naples, Corfu and Constantinople before returning to his native Venice. There he supported himself as a violinist and possibly as a magician.

Suspected by the **Inquisition** in 1749, Casanova fled to Lyon, where he joined the **Masonic order**, and then went on to Paris, Dresden, Prague and Vienna. During this six-year trek, Casanova supported himself mostly by gambling and won friends, lovers and influence with his charm.

Back in Venice, he was arrested as a magician and a **Freemason** and thrown in prison. Casanova escaped and went to Paris in 1757, where his introduction of the lottery secured his acceptance by the aristocracy. During his broad rambles through Europe, he was named **Chevalier (Knight) de Seingalt** in Holland, he met **Voltaire** (1694-1778) in Geneva and **Catherine the Great** (1729

**Giovanni Giacomo Casanova**

-1796) in St. Petersburg, while **Frederick II** (1712-1786) offered him a post in Berlin.

But trouble dogged Casanova's footsteps. He was expelled from Paris, Vienna and Florence, and also forced to leave Warsaw after a duel on the heels of a scandal. Allowed to return to Venice in 1774, Casanova served as a spy for Venetian inquisitors until 1782. His final years were spent as a librarian at the count's castle in Bohemia, where he penned his memoirs "to keep from going mad or dying from grief."

Casanova's lengthy autobiography, which offers a vivid picture of eighteenth century Europe, was first printed in German (1822-1828) and then in French (1826-1838). However, authorities doubted its authenticity and accuracy, and it was not until the twentieth century that the original manuscript was published in France as *Histoire de ma vie* (*History of My Life*, 1960-1962).

# 35. DANIEL BOONE
## 1734-1820

Even while he lived, **Daniel Boone** exemplified bravery, leadership and the freewheeling frontier spirit. A popular auto-biography (actually written by **John Filson**) had already appeared by 1784, and it circulated throughout America and abroad.

This famous explorer, Native American fighter and surveyor provided the inspiration for **James Fenimore Cooper**'s hero in *The Leatherstocking Tales* (1823-1841), and Lord **George Gordon Byron** gave him a tribute in *Don Juan* (1823). In 1905, Daniel Beard founded **The Society of the Sons of Daniel Boone**, which was later incorporated into **The Boy Scouts of America**.

When he was 21, Boone's curiosity was piqued when he heard about a hunter's paradise, the unexplored Kentucky. In 1769, Boone and five others followed the Warriors' Path through the Cumberland Gap into the state.

**Daniel Boone**

In 1775, Boone helped buy the lands between the Kentucky and Cumberland rivers from the **Cherokees** for a North Carolina judge, who was attempting to start a new colony. With 30 men, he then laid out the **Wilderness Road**, a trail that countless settlers would use to trek west. Boone also settled Boonesborough on the Kentucky River, just south of present-day Lexington. His wife and daughter were the first white women to see that part of the state.

During this time, Boone had two well-known conflicts with **Native Americans**. When his daughter **Jemina** and two of her friends were kidnapped, Boone rescued them unharmed. Later, he was captured and made into a brave by the **Shawnees**. After Boone learned they were going to attack his fort, he escaped and traveled the 160 miles (260 kilometers) in four days. Although the settlement was sieged for nine days, the Native Americans withdrew.

After serving as Boonesborough's legislator and in several other civic offices, Boone encountered problems with land titles and fell deeply into debt. So at the invitation of the Spanish governor who controlled Missouri, Boone brought a group of settlers there in 1799. When asked why he was leaving Kentucky, he replied "Too many people! Too crowded!" After the **Louisiana Purchase**, Boone would lose his lands there too.

There are numerous legends attributed to this folk hero. When some Native Americans surprised his party, Boone scared them away by convincing them that he had swallowed their scalping knife. Another tale claims when he knew he was near death, Boone took his favorite rifle, Tick-Licker, to a deer lick, where he died with the weapon cocked and his finger on the trigger.

42

**Paul Revere** has become an immortal American figure due to his midnight ride that carried the news that British troops were advancing on Concord and Lexington. The incident would never have become an integral part of US history if **Henry Wadsworth Longfellow** had never written the extremely popular poem, "Paul Revere's Ride" (1861).

Revere was born into a Boston family of French Huguenot descent. In 1756, he fought briefly as a second lieutenant in The French and Indian War, and then entered his father's silversmith business.

The craftsman subsequently immersed himself in several **Whig** groups and etched a number of well-received political cartoons. At **Samuel Adams'** (1722-1803) urging, Revere engraved a deliberate misrepresentation of **The Boston Massacre**, which angered many colonists onto the rebels' side.

In 1770, he started acting as an express (a mounted messenger). When English ships arrived with the tea that was to be taxed, Revere rode to other coastal cities to tell them not to let the British land their freight. Later, after being one of the "Indians" in the **Boston Tea Party**, he journeyed to Pennsylvania to spread the good news.

In the spring of 1775, the patriots learned that the British were going to arrest **John Hancock** (1737-1793) and Samuel Adams in Lexington and confiscate the Whigs' military supplies in Concord. Four days before the enemy expedition, Revere forewarned the colonists and arranged that a signal would be flashed from Boston's Old North Church: one lantern if the British were coming by land, and two if they were coming by sea.

On the evening of April 18th, Revere and **William Dawes** set out separately for Lexington, informing different areas of the countryside. At Lexington, Hancock and Adams fled, and Dr. **Samuel Prescott** joined Revere and Dawes. The three embarked for Concord, but stopped by a British patrol, only Prescott would reach the final destination. Revere, released without his borrowed horse, returned to Lexington for important papers in Hancock's trunk. When the redcoats arrived there the following morning, the minutemen were waiting.

In 1871, a city located about four miles (six kilometers) from Boston changed its name to Revere. Today his house still stands in downtown Boston, where it is the oldest existing structure, and visitors may view its authentic furnishings as well as the patriot hero's mementos.

**Paul Revere's famous ride.**

43

Like **Vlad the Impaler** (see no. 21), this man was the inspiration for one of the most chilling novels ever written. In **William Brodie**, **Robert Louis Stevenson** (1850- 1894) saw two diametrically opposed personalities in one body, each struggling for domination. His resulting book, *The Strange Case of Dr. Jeckyll and Mr. Hyde* (1886), is part thriller and part moral allegory.

While the story secured Stevenson's renown with the Victorian masses, its intriguing characters — the outwardly respectable Jeckyll and the odious Hyde — today remain as ominous a presence in the public's mind as Dracula or Frankenstein. By 1920, twelve silent film versions had already been released. Since then, **John Barrymore**, **Spencer Tracy** and **Boris Karloff** have played the mad scientist and his alter ego in literal adaptations and satires of the tale.

Like Dr. Jeckyll, Brodie was thought to be "a kind and goodly man, one of the noblest souls one could meet." He had a stately house and was a member of Edinborough's City Council. The short, dark-haired man with large brown eyes was also the **Deacon of Incorporation of Wrights**, which had to do with Brodie's master carpenter status, not with any organized religion.

However, Brodie established a pious reputation for himself by wearing white every day and frequently reading his Bible in public. A bachelor, he told friends that his quest to be the best cabinetmaker in town left no time for romance.

But Brodie secretly supported two mistresses and five illegitimate children. At night, dressed in black, he drank and gambled in the disreputable Fleshmarket area. This expensive lifestyle depleted Brodie's inheritance, and in 1768 he began a career of burglary that would span 20 years.

He copied the keys to the homes, banks and government buildings he legitimately worked in, and as he knew the police's patrol schedules, he could strike at unguarded times. Twice he was almost caught by acquaintances who saw a masked Brodie carrying a pistol, but they decided it could not have been the upstanding citizen they knew.

After these close calls, Brodie began to work with accomplices. Eventually, one of them supplied the names of the burglars to authorities. Brodie fled to Amsterdam and was preparing to migrate to America, but he was nabbed after a letter to one of his mistresses was intercepted.

Despite his confident manner and innocent demeanor, he was found guilty and sentenced to hang. A prison doctor then offered Brodie a plan to survive his execution. A silver tube would go in his throat to prevent strangulation, while wires to support his weight would be hidden beneath his clothes and attached to the rope by the bribed hangman.

On his execution day, the elegantly attired Brodie ignored both the crowd of 40,000 and the attending champlain. But the hangman did not bother with the wires, and although the doctor tried to resuscitate him for an hour, Brodie was truly dead.

**William Brodie.**

# BETSY ROSS
## 1752-1836

This colonial seamstress is reputed to have sewn the first American flag that had stars and stripes on it. This legend was not made public until 1870, when her grandson, **William J. Canby**, published the story that his 84-year-old grandmother had told him when he was eleven years old.

Because no proof has been found to verify Canby's claim, many historians have discounted it as a tall tale. Regardless, to most people, **Betsy Ross** is as much a folk hero as the other key figures in the United States' formative years.

**Elizabeth Griscom** was born to a **Quaker** family in Philadelphia, where she would remain for her entire life. After possibly attending the Friends School, at the age of 21 she eloped with **John Ross**, an upholsterer.

When her husband died in a munitions explosion three years later, Betsy took over his shop and became regarded in the area as an expert seamstress. During her career, she was the official flagmaker for the Pennsylvania Navy.

**Betsy Ross.**

Canby's story begins in June of 1776, when Betsy Ross received a visit from a committee that was headed by **George Washington** (1732-1799). One of the members of the group was John Ross' uncle, **George Ross** (1730-1799), whose conspicuously underlined signature is on the **Declaration of Independence**.

The men wanted Betsy to make the **"Stars and Stripes"** from a rough sketch they gave her. Up until that time, the revolutionaries had fought under local banners. Although General Washington wanted the 13 stars to have six points, she persuaded

him that they would look better with just five.

Even if the entire incident between Betsy Ross and the founding fathers never occurred, it is a marvelous part of the American folklore tradition. The flag that she may or may not have sewn was adopted by Congress on June 14, 1777.

Not much else is known about Betsy Ross, other than that she didn't have any better luck with her two subsequent husbands. **Joseph Ashburn** died in 1782, and **John Claypoole**, in 1817. In the course of these marriages, she gave birth to seven daughters. Betsy Ross retired from her business at age 75 and died on January 30, 1836.

This frivolous and double-dealing queen contributed to the unrest that caused the **French Revolution**, which left the monarchy overthrown and she and her husband beheaded. **Marie Antoinette** has become an emblem of an age in which the extravagances of those in power starkly contrasted the poverty-stricken existence of everyone else. Her personality is best characterized by the callous remark she is said to have made after hearing that the people had no bread: "Let them eat cake!" ("Qu'ils mangent de la brioche!")

A Vienna native, **Josèphe Jeanne Marie Antoinette** was born to the Austrian Emperor **Francis I** and Empress **Maria Theresa**. Her betrothal to the French dauphin (later **Louis XVI**; 1754-1793) was arranged to strengthen the alliance between the two countries.

When the pampered and vivacious Marie Antoinette arrived in **Versailles** at the age of 15, she had neither the education nor the attitude required for her tremendous role.

By 1774, when Louis XVI was crowned, Marie Antoinette was gambling, dancing and acting in amateur theatricals, socializing exclusively with like-minded aristocrats. Her many clothing and jewelry purchases eventually earned the powdered and pomaded queen the nickname "**Madame Deficit**," although she incurred only a small part of France's mammoth national debt.

Perceived by much of the snubbed court as an Austrian advocate, Marie Antoinette became the object of several slanderous pamphlets detailing her alleged extramarital affairs. Her reputation was permanently discredited by the **Diamond Necklace Affair of 1785-1786**, which instituted the widely believed but incorrect notion that the queen sold herself to a cardinal for a piece of jewelry.

A more mature Marie Antoinette emerged after her first child's birth in 1788,

**Marie Antoinette**

but her persistent opposition to reform made her even more of a revolutionary scapegoat. Three years later, she convinced her husband to flee Paris and join his loyal forces on France's eastern border. However, recognized in Varennes, they were taken back to the capital as virtual prisoners.

In desperation, the queen tried in vain to convince her brother, **Leopold II of Austria** (1747-1792), to amass troops on France's border to threaten the revolutionaries. Marie Antoinette favored the French declaration of war against Austria in early 1792, believing that an invasion would easily defeat the revolutionaries. To guarantee this, she gave Austria military secrets.

The uprising of August 10, 1792 that finally destroyed the monarchy was partly brought on by a suspicion of the queen's actions. Placed in solitary confinement, she endured her trial, in which she was convicted of "intrigues and secret dealings with foreign powers," with poise and strength. On October 16, 1793, Marie Antoinette was executed on the guillotine.

The bitter **Civil War** is one of America's darkest chapters, and the strong passions of the time are represented in the spunky story of **Barbara Hauer Frietchie**. As immortalized in the popular **John Greenleaf Whittier** poem, hers is a dramatic tale, one of principles being more important than death and humanity overcoming hostility.

Like the legends of **Betsy Ross** (see no. 38) or **John and Priscilla Alden** (see no. 29), it is disputed whether this incident ever happened. Regardless, its charm is undeniable, and it will always hold a prominent position in the violent mass of Civil War lore.

In 1862, Maryland was being held by a federal marshall, and the citizens of Frederick, the state's second largest city, were evenly divided in their loyalties to the North and South. Barbara Frietchie, the 95-year-old widow of a glovemaker, fiercely sided with the Union.

On September 10th, 55,000 Confederate troops, led by the generals **Robert E. Lee** (1807-1870) and **Thomas Jonathan "Stonewall" Jackson** (1824-1863), passed through Frederick en route to the Battle of Antietam at Sharpsburg. One observer said that it took sixteen hours for the ragged army to pass through the town's streets. The battle they would fight a week later would mark the bloodiest single day in the entire war.

Whittier's "Barbara Frietchie" (1863) describes the aged patriot hanging a Union flag out of her attic window "to show that one heart was loyal yet." When Stonewall Jackson sees it, he orders his men to shoot it down. They do so, and she immediately restores it.

Barbara Frietchie's declaration to Jackson is the poem's most famous lines: " 'Shoot, if you must, this old gray head, But spare your country's flag,' she said."

Jackson's reaction is equally memorable: "The nobler nature within him stirred/ To life at that woman's deed and word: 'Who touches a hair of yon gray head/ Dies like a dog! March on!' he said."

Despite reports that Barbara Frietchie was bed-ridden that day and that she really waved the flag at the Union troops who marched through town two days later, Frederick remembers her as one of its most outstanding citizens. Whittier's poem is engraved on her tombstone in Mt. Olivet Cemetery, and a reproduction of her home sits on its original site as a museum.

**Barbara Hauer Frietchie.**

# MIKE FINK
## c. 1770-1822

During his lifetime, this legendary figure earned the title "the King of the Keelboatmen," Stories of his boastful nature, skilled marksmanship, madcap adventures and untimely death proliferated until the **Civil War**, first orally and then in print, obscuring the man's actual life.

Born near Fort Pitt (today's Pittsburgh), it is said that as a child **Mike Fink** was so adept with a Kentucky rifle that he was banned from shooting matches. At 17, he became a scout on Western Pennsylvania's dangerous frontier, protecting forts from British and Native American attacks. Fink then worked on keelboats in the Ohio and Mississippi rivers, a hardy job that required navigating the slender boats upstream. The rugged keelboatmen, known as "half-horse, half-alligator" men, were renowned for their brawling, bragging, drinking and prowess with the ladies. Fink outdid all the others in these pursuits, earning himself the privilege of wearing a red feather in his hat that proclaimed him king bully of the river. He claimed to be able to drink a gallon of whiskey a day without staggering. The red-haired man supposably left illegitimate children wherever he went, and any

**Mike Fink**

red-haired child was dubbed "Mike Fink's brat" by other boatmen.

Most tales about Fink occur within this period and involve his cruel pranks. In one, he shoots the scalp lock off a Native American named **Proud Joe** for fun. The keelboat is ambushed by the Native American tribe that night, but Fink kills Proud Joe in the dark.

The boatman was even linked with another American hero, **Davy Crockett** (see no. 46). In one anecdote, Fink, in an alligator skin, attempts to scare Crockett's wife by pouncing on her. After cutting his disguise open with her "Arkansas toothpick," or **Bowie knife**, she flogs him with her bare hands. Another tale, printed in *Davy Crockett's Almanack* (1839), has Fink beating Crockett in a shooting match after the two exchange boasts in the finest frontier slang.

When the steamboats that Fink is said to have hated so much began replacing keelboats, he joined the **Ashley-Henry fur expedition** to the upper Missouri River region as a boatman and trapper. The following year he was murdered, probably at the mouth of the Yellowstone River.

Varying accounts of his death mostly agree that Fink accidently killed a man with his rifle, "Bang-all" or "Old Bets," while playing his favorite game, shooting a tin cup from someone's head. A friend of the deceased then fired on Fink. Most stories add that his murderer died a few weeks later while trying to cross a river.

After Fink's death, several writers immediately deified him, comparing him to **Hercules**, **William Tell** (see no. 18), and **Casanova** (see no. 34). Yet he also became regarded as a backwoods bogey-man, and parents used him to make their children behave. One Missouri superstition claims that Mike Fink did not die at all, but turned himself into a huge catfish that starts floods and storms by moving his tail.

# 42. JOHNNY APPLESEED
## c. 1774-1845

This freewheeling eccentric is credited with spreading apple orchards from the Allegheny River to the Saint Marys River. **John Chapman**'s altruistic life has become practically indistinguishable from the **Johnny Appleseed legend**, which developed during the time when more enterprising men were seeking their fortunes in the unexplored western lands.

For 48 years that began in 1797, Chapman traveled alone through Ohio and Indiana, planting as he wandered and returning later for pruning, earning a unforgettable reputation from the start. Dubbing himself Johnny Appleseed, he gave apple seeds and saplings to everyone he met, usually refusing money. When his seeds were gone, he got a fresh supply from an apple cider mill instead of wastefully cutting down a tree to procure them.

In his path, Chapman also left several healing herbs, including dog fennel or mayweed, which he erroneously believed to be a cure for malaria. When he met and befriended **Native Americans**, they considered him a white medicine man.

Johnny Appleseed preached the theology of **Swedenbourgianism**, and his simple life exemplified the true primitive Christian. His shirt was a coffee sack, and a tin pan on his head was used for his cooking. When Chapman couldn't find any castoff boots, he went barefoot. One legend describes how, on a snowy day, a man forced Johnny Appleseed to accept a pair of shoes. A few days later, the two met again, and Chapman was again shoeless. When asked why, Chapman explained that he had encountered a poor family who needed them more than he.

**Johnny Appleseed.**

Another popular tale about Johnny Appleseed has led to his being dubbed "a Frontier **Paul Revere**" (see no. 36). During the War of 1812, Mansfield, Ohio was under siege by Native Americans. Chapman saved the town by running barefoot through the night to get help from Mt. Vernon, 30 miles (48 kilometers) away. On his way, he blasted on his powder horn to alert isolated settlements and families of the danger.

Chapman died near Fort Wayne, Indiana, where today a city park and several other monuments pay tribute to his unmarked grave. Several novels, short stories and poems posthumously recorded the folk tales about him. One of the most well known articles to describe his deeds, **W.D. Haley**'s "Johnny Appleseed, a Pioneer Hero" (1871), appeared in *Harper's New Monthly Magazine*.

Like **Captain Kidd** (see no. 31), **Jean Laffite** is considered to be a privateer turned pirate, and several folk legends about his hidden treasure also abound. At the height of his career, the shrewd and handsome Frenchman is said to have controlled nearly all the import traffic of the lower Mississippi valley.

By 1810, the republic of Cartagena (now Colombia) had commissioned the adventurer to be a privateer on Spanish ships. Operating from a base on a secluded island in Barataria Bay, just south of New Orleans, Laffite smuggled the pilfered goods and slaves into the city, with his blacksmith shop there serving as a cover.

In September of 1814, the British offered Laffite $30,000 in gold and a captaincy in the **Royal Navy** if he would help them invade New Orleans. He pretended to agree, but then notified the Louisiana governor of the danger and volunteered the aid of his illicit forces.

Instead of accepting Laffite's proposal, the governor sent the military to destroy the Barataria colony and arrest the entire band. Some of the smuggler's ships were captured, but his operation remained intact.

Laffite then offered his group's services to Major General **Andrew Jackson** (1767-1845) if they all got a full pardon. Jackson, in dire need of troops who could handle hostile fire, accepted.

During the **Battle of New Orleans** (December 1814 - January 1815), Laffite and his crew fought notably well. Jackson called the leader "one of the ablest men" of the campaign, and President **James Madison** issued a public pardon for the entire group.

Although he was embraced by New Orleans society, Laffite returned to his old ways. In 1817, he sailed to Galveston Island and built a base called **Campeche**. Laffite would later boast that he buried enough money there to build a solid gold bridge across the Mississippi River.

Jean Laffite.

From Campeche, Laffite, along with his 13 ships and his 1,000 followers, openly preyed on the Spanish colonial ships in the name of the Mexican revolutionary flag. But his lieutenants attacked American ships, and a US warship entered the pirate base in 1819. Although he extravagantly entertained the commander, Laffite was ordered to abandon the colony.

Laffite loaded his goods onto his favorite brig, the *Pride*, burned Campeche down, and left. He was later reported to have appeared in several places. Conflicting accounts have Laffite dying in the Yucatan peninsula in 1825, of tropical fever in 1826, or during a conflict with a British warship in the Gulf of Mexico.

In the ensuing years, almost every inlet or island along the Gulf coast was considered a possible site for the adventurer's mythical treasure. His ghost is also said to wander the earth, searching for someone who will use it for good as opposed to selfish purposes. Only when he finds that person will Jean Laffite be absolved of his sins.

# 44. SIMÓN BOLÍVAR
## 1783-1830

Called **El Libertador** (**The Liberator**) and "the **George Washington of South America**," this illustrious general and dictator played a major role in expelling Spanish colonial rule from northern South America. Later, with power extending from the Caribbean to the Argentine-Bolivian border, **Simón Bolívar**'s downfall occurred as the result of numerous conflicts amongst his republics.

Born to a wealthy Caracas family, The Liberator was orphaned young and sent to study in Europe at age 16. When his Spanish bride died of yellow fever shortly after their arrival in Caracas, the heartbroken Bolívar returned to Europe. From the heights of Monte Sacro in Rome, he vowed to free his land from imperialist rule.

After establishing a base in Angostura in Venezuela, The Liberator conceived his daring takeover of New Granada (now Colombia). By leading about 2,500 men through flood-swept plains and over the icy Andes, Bolívar surprised the Spanish. In the **Battle of Boyacá** in August of 1819, Colombia was liberated.

He then returned to Angostura to be made president and military dictator of the Republic of Gran Colombia, which included Colombia, Venezuela, and Ecuador. Two of its components were still controlled by the Spanish, but by the end of 1822, both countries were emancipated. It was in Ecuador that Bolívar met his great passion, **Manuela Sáenz**.

Under The Liberator's best general, **Antonio José de Sucre** (c. 1795-1830), the Spanish lost Peru in 1824, and Bolívar was made its dictator as well. The following year, upper Peru declared its independence as Bolivia, and its namesake president wrote its constitution.

Bolívar then attempted to realize another dream, that of solidarity amongst all of South America's nations. But the impoverished republics were sharply divided racially and socially, and fought both internally and with each other.

Bolívar persuaded Venezuela and Ecuador not to secede, and then quelled insurrections in Colombia and Peru. Forced to retain his empire with might, his popularity plummeted. A murder attempt in Bogotá was only averted due to Sáenz' quick wits.

In 1829, Bolívar and Sucre thwarted a Peruvian invasion of Ecuador and then crushed a revolt led by one their most honored generals. The following year, Venezuela and Ecuador seceded from Gran Colombia.

Disappointed and ill, Bolívar resigned on April 27. Planning to return to Europe, Bolivar cancelled those plans when Sucre, his intended successor, was assassinated. The Liberator died later that year in the Santa Marta house of an admirer who, ironically, was Spanish.

**Simón Bolívar**

51

Like **Aesop's fables** (see no. 5) or **Mother Goose's rhymes** (see no. 32), the folk tales collected and published by **Jakob and Wilhelm Grimm** have become childhood institutions. Like characters in their stories, **The Brüder Grimm**, as they are known in their native Germany, had personalities that balanced each other out, and their important collaborations extended throughout their lives.

Born in Hanau, both brothers attended the University of Marburg. Jakob was more scholarly, with sharp features and a short, slender stature. The taller Wilhelm, who had a severe heart disorder, was more lighthearted and outgoing. He would marry and raise a family, while the bachelor Jakob would travel extensively for research purposes.

After Jakob worked as a librarian and Wilhelm as a secretary in Kassel, the brothers went to Göttingen in 1830, where they each held the post of librarian and professor. In 1837, they were fired for protesting the new king's constitution. At an invitation from **Frederick William IV** (1795-1861), the king of Prussia, the brothers went to Berlin to lecture at the **Royal Academy of Sciences**.

**The Brothers Grimm.**

There they continued writing several groundbreaking volumes in the fields of historical linguistics (the study of language) and Germanic philology (the study of written records). Wilhelm stayed in Berlin, while Jacob researched throughout Europe. Both would die in Berlin, and the brothers are buried there.

*Kinder- und Hausmärchen* (*Child and House Tales?*; 1812-1815, 1819-1822) contained 200 tales, some of which date back to the sixteenth century. Jakob exactingly selected and arranged the stories, which came from mostly oral sources, while Wilhelm gave them their readable form without altering their content. The book was later translated into English as *Grimm's Fairy Tales* (1844), and it can now be read in 70 languages.

The stories, which have been critically dubbed "nightmarish" and "irrational and unnatural," nevertheless possess a certain charm. The protagonist's virtue is always rewarded, while evil never goes unpunished. The captivating tales also feature profuse magic and spells of enchantment, as well as communication between animals and humans.

For example, the story of Tom Thumb tells of a clever peasant boy who is the size of a thumb. To help his parents financially, he convinces them to sell him to two greedy men. Before returning home, Tom thwarts a robbery and is swallowed by a cow and then by a wolf.

Some of the most familiar tales of the Brothers Grimm include: "Sleeping Beauty," "Hansel and Gretel," "Rumpelstiltskin," "Rapunzel," "Cinderella," "Snow White" and "The Seven Dwarfs," "Red Riding Hood" and "The Golden Goose." Almost all of these have been turned into plays, films, or animated features, with the most popular cartoons being those produced by **Walt Disney Studios** (see no. 88).

# DAVY CROCKETT
## 1786-1836

**Davy Crockett** was famous during his lifetime as a charismatic backwater politician, but his death at the **Alamo** made him a national hero. As one of the most enduring symbols of the American frontier, he has been the subject of paintings, songs, books, TV programs and films.

Born in Tennessee, Crockett played hooky often, becoming a cattle-driver at 12 and a wagoner at 14. At 16, he hired himself out for 18 months to help his father with a $76 debt.

Crockett was later a US Army scout and fought in the **Creek Indian War**. In 1817, Crockett took his family to Tennessee and launched his political career. Throughout it, his humorous speeches would contain backwoods brags, such as that he once killed 105 bears in eight months.

After serving two terms in the state legislature, Crockett began two congressional terms as a **Democrat** in 1827. Always a champion of the working class and underdogs, he bitterly broke with President **Andrew Jackson** (1767-1845) over bills concerning land reform and relocating **Native American** tribes.

Defeated in 1831, Crockett switched allegiance to the **Whigs**, who took the outspoken politician on a successful speaking tour. He won another term in 1833, but lost his next reelection bid, and talk of making him the Whigs' 1836 presidential candidate ceased.

Crockett was so resentful of Jackson that he "seceded" from the Union, taking a small band of volunteers with him to Texas, then fighting for independence from Mexico. In 1836, they joined the forces who were preparing to defend the Alamo against the Mexican army.

Although greatly outnumbered by the 2,400 Latin American forces, Crockett and the 187 others defended the Alamo for nearly two weeks. On March 6, the Mexican army overran the compound, killing all the men there.

Even before the tragedy, Crockett was the subject of many newspaper articles, and books and magazines, such as *Davy Crockett's Almanack* (started in 1834), were printing tall tales about him. People, animals, steamboats and locomotive engines were also being named for him.

In the wake of the fall of the Alamo, however, Crockett's popularity snowballed. In Texas, a city, a county and a national park bear his name, and many legends about his actions at the Alamo were born.

Davy Crockett is said to have died defending the area in front of the chapel with his rifle Betsy, four pistols and a **Bowie knife**, which is named for fellow Alamo victim **James "Jim" Bowie** (1799-1836)]. "Won't you come into my bower?" he sang as he greeted the Mexicans. While most people believed he died fighting, there are a few who think the cunning Davy Crockett escaped.

**Davy Crockett.**

# 47. HANS CHRISTIAN ANDERSEN
## 1805-1875

The fairy tales of **Hans Christian Andersen** are famous throughout the world with children and adults alike. Indeed, they are some of the most frequently translated stories in all of history.

Like a character in a **Horatio Alger** (see no. 55) novel, Andersen would break through the unyielding social structure of his time to succeed beyond his wildest dreams. He was born in a slum in Denmark, the son of a poor shoemaker and his superstitious wife. When Andersen was 14, he went to Copenhagen to become an actor, a dancer or a singer.

Andersen eventually performed at the **Royal Theater**, but left when his voice changed. With little formal education, he started writing plays for the theater, but they were all rejected. Then a director there raised money to send the young man to grammar school.

Andersen was miserable living in the home of the headmaster, a cruel bully, but he was able to enter the **University of Copenhagen** in 1828. Starting in 1827, his poems, plays, novels, autobiographies and travel sketches began to be published, receiving acclaim throughout Europe.

However, it is Andersen's 168 fairy tales that made his name. Published between 1835 and 1872, they were groundbreaking in their field, breaking with literary tradition by borrowing the familiar slang of spoken language. By combining his imaginative storytelling methods with elements common to folk tales throughout the world, Andersen assured that his stories would be quickly embraced wherever they might be read.

Because they have many different levels of meaning, the stories also interest adults. The tree in "The Fir Tree" can represent a certain attitude of not appreciating your blessings, while the toy soldier in "The Steadfast Tin Soldier" can be seen as a resoluteness in the face of destiny's pitfalls. Yet the tales still manage to appeal to a child's sense of wonder and curiosity.

Despite his outward success, the extremely sensitive Andersen still perceived himself as an outsider or an outcast. This element runs through his tales and is part of what makes them so powerful. Thus in "The Little Match Girl," the cold loneliness of the girl during the Christmas season was probably experienced in some form by the writer. While that story ends quite bleakly, others, such as "The Snow Queen," end with good overcoming evil.

Other popular tales include: "The Emperor's New Clothes," "The Red Shoes," "The Nightingale," "The Princess and the Pea," "Thumbelina," "The Tinderbox," "The Ugly Duckling," and "The Little Mermaid." Many of these have been adapted into unforgettable animated features and touching motion pictures. Today children regularly sit on the lap of a huge bronze statue of Hans Christian Andersen in New York City's Central Park.

**Hans Christian Andersen.**

# 48. KIT CARSON
## 1809-1868

**Daniel Boone** (see no. 35) explored east of the Mississippi River, but **Kit Carson** trail-blazed the lands west of it. This skillful hunter, guide and soldier was short, quiet-spoken and bandy-legged, but his legends have made him six feet tall, with the physique of Hercules and a loud, booming voice.

**Christopher Carson**'s parents were restless wanderers heading west from North Carolina. Their son was born in Madison, Kentucky, and the next year the family settled in Howard County in Missouri.

Kit had no formal education, and at about the age of 15 he was apprenticed to a saddlemaker. He hated it, and later ran away with a group of traders headed for Santa Fe.

From 1829 until 1842, Carson worked as a fur trapper in Arizona, California, Idaho and Wyoming, finally lodging in the Rocky Mountains. On numerous occasions, he fought horse and fur thieves as well as antagonistic Native Americans and trappers.

Many folk tales about Carson occur during this period of his life. One describes a duel he fought with a French trapper named **Shuman**, who offended Kit by calling Americans "scullions and chicken-livered scoundrels." The two rode at each other shooting from 100 yards apart. A whizzing bullet snipped a lock of hair from Carson's head, but he then lodged a humbling bullet in the Frenchman's elbow.

Carson, however, gained renown in his lifetime as a skilled guide for three expeditions led by a government explorer, Lieutenant **John Charles Frémont** (1813-1890). Often traversing hostile Native American lands, the journeys safely passed through a large chunk of the west.

When the **Mexican War** broke out in 1846, the group went to California to fight. After a victorious battle, a party led by Car-

**Kit Carson.**

son was dispatched to Washington, DC to spread the news. But in New Mexico, they met a general who ordered them to guide his troops back to California.

When the group was attacked by Mexicans, Carson and two others slipped through enemy lines to get help in San Diego, walking and crawling the 30 miles (48 kilometers), and the American troops were saved. He then completed his original duty in a phenomenally short time.

In 1861, at the opening of the **Civil War**, he was made colonel of the New Mexico Volunteers Regiment. At the **Battle of Valverde**, Carson fought the Confederates, and later clashed with the **Apache, Navajo, Kiowa,** and **Comanche** tribes. His greatest military coup came in the 1864 **Battle of Adobe Walls** in Texas, when his 400 troops routed between 1,500 and 3,000 Native Americans.

After being made a brigadier general, Carson took command of Colorado's Fort Garland in 1864. He would resign the following year due to illness, and die the year after that. Today Nevada's capital city eternally pays tribute to its brave namesake.

With outrageous deceptions and melodramatic publicity, this showman completely changed the face of entertainment and became a celebrity in the process. Credited with originating the phrase, "There's a sucker born every minute," the shrewd and imaginative **P. T. Barnum** was one of the minds behind "The Greatest Show on Earth." It was the biggest, most monumental and most celebrated circus that there had ever been, and the fabulous spectacle still tours today.

Phineas Taylor Barnum's career began in New York City in 1835, when he exhibited his first hoax, a woman touted as the 161-year-old former nurse of **George Washington**. He followed this with more deceptions as well as authentic oddities, such as the famous Siamese twins, **Chang and Eng Bunker**.

In 1842, he opened **Barnum's American Museum**. By the time it closed 26 years later, Barnum's various enterprises had drawn 82 million visitors, including **Henry James** and **Edward VII**.

In 1842, he also discovered his most lucrative exhibit yet, a 25-inch-tall, 5-year-old midget named **Charles Stratton** (see no. 57). Barnum, borrowing the title of a **Brothers Grimm tale** (see no. 45), renamed the precocious child **General Tom Thumb**.

Barnum next risked his fortune to bring **Jenny Lind**, a singer he had neither seen or heard, to the United States. Dubbing the soprano "**the Swedish Nightingale**" in his

**P.T. Barnum.**

biggest publicity campaign yet, her national tour earned critical acclaim and a tidy profit.

Barnum, whose tall height, bulbous nose and potbelly lent him a memorable appearance, built a three-story Oriental mansion, Iranistan, in Bridgeport, Connecticut. There he entertained such guests **Mark Twain** (see no. 56) and the journalist **Horace Greeley** (1811-1872).

In 1855, however, a bad investment left Barnum bankrupt. Taking some of his acts on a European tour helped financially, and there he discovered that people were just as eager to gape at him. Barnum now began lucratively lecturing on such topics as "The Art of Money-Getting."

In 1881, Barnum and **James A. Bailey** created "The Greatest Show on Earth." Its first scandal was centered around the acquisition of **Jumbo**, reputed to be the world's largest elephant, from the **London Zoo**. After the purchase was finalized, Queen **Victoria** and the *London Times* demanded that the contract be broken, creating a huge bout of publicity. Barnum later estimated that Jumbo earned him $300,000 in six weeks.

At the age of 81, Barnum's health began to decline. At his request, a New York newspaper printed his obituary early so that he might enjoy it. When he died two weeks later, the *London Times* wrote, "His name is a proverb already, and a proverb it will continue to be."

This young man's identity is one of the greatest unsolved mysteries of the nineteenth century. From the moment of his appearance until his enigmatic death, **Kaspar Hauser, the Mystery Man of Europe**, left only questions in his path. These have since inspired a play, a film and several novels.

In 1828, a youth stumbled into Nuremberg with two letters for a military captain. He answered questions with "Weiss nicht" - "I don't know," but he could write his name. His documents later proved to have been penned by the same disguised hand. The first purported to be from a laborer who raised him, but had never let him go outside. The second was supposably written by Hauser's mother to the laborer, asking him to care for the child, and when he was grown, to take him to the captain, with whom the boy's dead father had served.

Hauser had indeed been confined for most of his life. His skin was unnaturally pale, and his feet were so tender, they bled through his shoes. His mentality was that of a three-year-old, and Hauser was first thought to be retarded.

**Kaspar Hauser**

Jailed as a vagrant, Hauser grew more alert each day, nourished by the attention of his many visitors. His vocabulary increased, and his features grew more intelligent. Hauser's only deformity was that he had protrusions on the backs of his knees, making him walk clumsily.

Hauser explained that he grew up in a small room without light. He never saw anyone, as his food was left while he slept. One day a man appeared, taught Hauser to write his name and say a few phrases, and left him at the city's gates.

The town council appointed a guardian to tutor him and offered a reward for clues to his identity. A criminologist developed the intriguing theory that Hauser must be of royal blood, and then someone tried to kill the mystery man. While a few people believed that Hauser did it himself, most agreed his life was in danger.

Then a wealthy English lord took Hauser to many of Europe's minor courts. However, all this attention made him quite egotistical, and the lord deposited him in the small town of Ansbach, about 25 miles away from Nuremberg. Hauser hated it there, and he was soon attacked again. He said he had gotten a message to go to a park, where a man had stabbed him in the side. However, there was only one set of footprints in the snow. Before slipping into a coma, Hauser's last words were, "I didn't do it myself."

After his death, a deluge of pamphlets and books circulated, each containing fanciful speculations on Hauser's ancestry. Though the name was never actually printed, the most popular candidates were the Grand Dukes of Baden. The elderly Duke Karl Frederick had married an 18-year-old, and she supposably got rid of his other children so that her own would be titled. This was denied by the family, and like every theory, there is no evidence to support or disprove it.

# 51. DR. DAVID LIVINGSTONE
## 1813-1873

Over a 30-year span of time, this dedicated explorer made several important expeditions into Africa, becoming an international celebrity and setting the stage for the continent's colonization. During Dr. **David Livingstone**'s final journey, in which he unsuccessfully searched for the elusive source of the **Nile River**, the world was so concerned about the missing doctor that an American newspaper dispatched Sir **Henry Morton Stanley** (1841-1904) to search for him. When he was found, he was greeted with the now-famous phrase, "Dr. Livingstone, I presume?"

Livingstone was born in a Scottish ghetto and bought a Latin grammar book with his first week's wages from a cotton mill. Ordained as a missionary in 1840, he journeyed to Africa the following year with his lifelong maxim of **Christianity**, commerce and civilization.

**Dr. David Livingstone.**

Between 1841 and 1856, Livingstone made several crucial breakthroughs. He traveled further into Kalahari country than any white man before him, established a non-slavery trade route from the African interior to the Atlantic coast, and named **Victoria Falls** for his queen. Returning to England a national hero, his *Missionary Travels and Researches in South Africa* (1857) immediately sold 70,000 copies.

Livingstone was then appointed British consul and embarked on an expedition to explore several rivers and lakes. However, many mishaps occurred. His wife died on the Zambezi river, and his son, who was to join him, was killed fighting for the North in the **Civil War**. Livingstone fought with and dismissed some accompanying Europeans. The expedition was cancelled in 1863, although later it would become apparent that several important findings had been made.

Back in Britain, Livingstone, prematurely weak from his strenuous travels, was advised to get surgery, but he refused. Returning to Africa in 1866, his goal was to find the start of the Nile. Livingstone quarreled with his African and Asian followers, and several defected, one with his medical supplies. To avoid punishment, they said the doctor had died, and this circulated abroad.

The expedition discovered two lakes and reached **Lake Tanganyika**, but Livingstone became quite ill. Meanwhile, nothing had been heard from him in two years, and Stanley tracked him down in 1871. The doctor recovered and explored 200 miles eastward with him. However, so obsessed was he by the origin of the Nile that he refused to leave Africa. In May of 1873, Livingstone died in today's Zambia. His heart was buried there, and it took nine months for his body to be carried to the coast. The doctor was buried in **Westminster Abbey** after a regal funeral.

With no formal legal training except his own criminal background, Judge **Roy Bean** represented "the law west of the Pecos" for just over 20 years. Most of the amusing folk tales about the bearded judge's bizarre manner of dispensing justice are supposed to have actually occurred.

Born to a poor Kentucky family, Bean set out for Mexico as a teenager. Forced to flee after killing a Mexican cowboy, he settled in California, where he ran a saloon and was a **California Ranger**. Bean later said that he'd left San Diego because he had killed a man in a horseback duel.

During the **Civil War**, Bean led a gang, the Free Rovers. They claimed to be a band of **Robin Hoods** (see no. #), stealing from the Union to give to the Confederates, but they were perceived as common thieves. After the war, Bean embarking on one failed money-making scheme after another. He filed several losing lawsuits, and the nearly illiterate man became acquainted with legal procedures. Bean also married, but his child bride left him.

On August 2, 1882, Bean was appointed justice of the peace in Langtry, Texas, a small isolated settlement on the Southern Pacific rail line. He claimed he named the town after the popular actress **Lily Langtry**, "the Jersey Lily." Bean called his 20-by-14-foot shack just that — but the sign outside was misspelled by a drunk working off his fine. Other signs read "LAW WEST OF THE PECOS" and "ICE BEER." Inside, a wrinkled picture of Langtry, the subject of countless toasts, hung behind the bar.

From the start, Bean was a unique judge, with justice often serving his own ends. The most famous story concerns a corpse brought to Bean. Finding $40 and a pistol in its pockets, Bean pocketed the money on a concealed weapons charge. He always made sure everyone bought "a good snort" before legal proceedings, but if anyone got drunk in the courtroom and not in the saloon, he was fined. Bean's eccentric wedding ceremonies concluded with the jurist looking into the groom's eyes and saying "May God have mercy on your soul," a statement usually reserved for death sentences.

By the start of the 20th century, Bean's colorful and unconventional reputation had traveled east, and hundreds came to observe him at work. Soon after his death from an extended drinking binge, Lily Langtry visited the shack. As a souvenir, she was given Judge Bean's pet bear, but it ran off, so she received his revolver instead.

**Judge Roy Bean.**

Dubbed "the Napoleon of the Indian race," **Geronimo** was a mighty **Apache** warrior whose assaults against the white man were some of the last of their kind. His life was a series of attacks and captures, and by the time of his final surrender, he was an established celebrity.

Geronimo was of the Nednais, a southern tribe of Chiricahua Apaches in Chihuahua, Mexico. Originally called **Goyathlay**, "the smart one," the Mexicans named him their word for Jerome. He first became a chieftain in 1858, when during a surprise attack, Mexican troops murdered his mother, wife and children. Geronimo was moved to an eastern Arizona reservation in 1871, but due to raids on settlers, the Chiricahuas were relocated five years later. The hated San Carlos Reservation was on a desolate tract of land in the east central part of the state.

Geronimo escaped and fought US troops in both Mexico and America, but was recaptured and returned to the reservation. A few years later he fled with a small group and established several hidden bases in Mexico's Sierra Madre mountains. From these, Geronimo led several violent raids on both sides of the border and successfully dodged the law from both nations. In May 1883 they surrendered to General **George Crook** (1829-1890), and were taken to another reservation.

All was quiet for a while, but Geronimo and a small band escaped yet again and restarted their former activities. American troops were sent on an intense campaign to recapture them, and their leader consented to a truce with Cook. Geronimo changed his mind and fled to Mexico, but capitulated in August 1886. Eight years later, he and his tribe, all prisoners of war, were moved first to Florida and then to Fort Sill, Oklahoma.

Utilizing his renown, Geronimo billed himself as an entertainment attraction, selling souvenir bows and arrows as well as pictures of himself at many public events. He appeared at the **St. Louis World's Fair** and attended the 1905 presidential inauguration of **Theodore Roosevelt** (1858-1919). When Geronimo was nearing death from pneumonia in Fort Sill, it is said that he refused to lie on a bed, preferring the earth from whence he came.

With the passage of nearly a century, all Americans have come to perceive Geronimo as more of tragic hero than an aggressor, as seen several sympathetic novels, films and TV shows based on him. During **World War II**, US Army Paratroopers began yelling his name as they alighted from aircraft. Today "Geronimo" is a popular slang term, shouted just before a daring jump.

Geronimo.

**Wild Bill Hickok** is remembered as one of the mightiest lawmen of the Old West, one who lived and died by the gun. The handsome sharpshooter's exploits, from Union spy to performer in **Buffalo Bill Cody's Wild West show** (see no. 61), were already legendary by the time of his death.

In his Illinois youth, James Butler Hickok assisted his father in transporting runaway slaves on the underground railroad. He went to Kansas in 1855, joining an anti-slavery gang called the **Redlegs**. A stint as constable in Monticello was followed by one as a stagecoach driver on the Santa Fe and Oregon trails. During this time, he and Buffalo Bill became good friends.

In Rock Creek, Nebraska, a controversial gun battle made Hickok famous. **David McCanles**, angered at Hickok for dating his girl-friend, was possibly shot after entering Hickok's cabin with a six-gun. However, other versions claim that McCanles was unarmed or that he was killed from behind a curtain while he shouted "Come out and fight fair!"

During the **Civil War**, Hickok was a spy and may have fought in the 1862 **Battle of Pea Ridge** in Arkansas. He probably earned his famous sobriquet around this time, perhaps after saving a youth from a lynch mob. In 1865, another celebrated shootout occurred in Springfield, Missouri, with **David Tutt**, again over a woman. As the men advanced on each other, Hickok warned his opponent not come any closer, and when this was ignored, Tutt was shot in the heart.

After being as a scout in **Custer**'s Seventh Cavalry (see no. 58), Hickok was sheriff of the violent Hays City in Kansas. While trying to make arrests, he killed three drunk men with his 1851 Navy Colts. This cemented Wild Bill's reputation for bravery and unerring aim, and he was invited to become marshal of the rough town of Abilene, Kansas in 1871. He bested some of the most feared badmen on the frontier, but became disenchanted after he accidentally shot a friend. It is said Hickok never again fired at anyone.

He briefly toured with Buffalo Bill Cody's show, astounding audiences with his marksmanship. Wild Bill disliked having to "play act" for a living, so during a gold rush, he moved to Deadwood, South Dakota, and supposably had a premonition that this would be his final home.

In a card game, he won $110 from **Jack McCall**, a cross-eyed laborer. Although Hickok lent him money for breakfast, the defeated man swore revenge. The following day, Wild Bill was playing poker in Saloon No. 10 with friends. He was facing the door and asked to exchange seats with one of the others, but was refused. McCall entered the saloon and shot the hero in the back. Wild Bill was dead by the time he hit the floor, and his cards, a pair of black aces and black eights, is known to this day as "**the Dead Man's Hand**."

**Wild Bill Hickok.**

# 55. HORATIO ALGER
## 1832-1899

**Horatio Alger** helped institute a wide-spread form of the American dream: the idea that with dedication and virtue, anyone could rise to the top. He was a childhood fixture to millions of young boys, who devoured his umpteen rags-to-riches books and dared to dream. Although both his work and his character have come under attack, his theme is a national ideal that continues to be copied and modified in TV and film dramas. A public figure who suddenly rises to fame from obscurity, as **Elvis Presley** (see no. 100) did, is quickly dubbed a Horatio Alger hero.

The son of a **Unitarian** minister, Alger graduated with honors from **Harvard University** at age 20. At his fathers' desire, he earned a degree from Harvard's Divinity School. In 1864, Alger was ordained and became the minister of an Unitarian church in Brewster, Massachusetts. Two years later, a scandal concerning local youths forced him to resign. Alger moved to New York City and became involved with the **Newsboys'**

**Lodging Home**, and its urchin residents became the inspiration for his stories.

His first literary undertaking, *Ragged Dick; or, Street Life in New York with the Bootblacks* (serialized in 1867, published as book in 1868), was a tremendous success from the moment it was published. It is the tale of an impoverished but virtuous shoeshine boy in New York City, who, with a bit of miraculous luck, is catapulted into wealth. For the next 30 years, Alger would stick to this storyline. In all, his 135 books would sell over 20 million copies, with the *Ragged Dick*, *Luck and Pluck*, and *Tattered Tom* series being the most popular.

Alger's work is rife with weak plots, unrealistic characters, and formal dialogue that is often ridiculously out of place. However, he was in the right place at the right time. In the latter part of the nineteenth century, monumental fortunes were being made in America's blossoming industrial cities, and the showy affairs of the rich and famous, like **Diamond Jim Brady** (see no. 66), were front-page news. Alger's stories thus held an irresistible appeal to the young, enabling them to envision a similar future for themselves.

Alger supported many charitable institutions for orphans and runaways. His goal to write fiction for adults was never realized, and he died a few years after returning to Massachusetts.

**Horatio Alger.**

# 56. **MARK TWAIN**
## 1835-1910

**Mark Twain**'s writing made him a literary giant, and his charisma made him an American institution. The cigar-smoking man in the white suit entertained as he enlightened, and his gruff speeches drew huge crowds. A truly fascinating character, he is said to have correctly predicted that his death, like his birth, would occur during the year of **Halley's Comet**.

**Samuel Langhorne Clemens** became captivated with river life while growing up in Hannibal, Missouri. In the 1850s, he began writing humorous pieces with pen names like "Thomas Jefferson Snodgrass" and "W. Epaminandos Adrastus Blab." At 21, he adopted the life of a steamboat pilot on the Mississippi River. Twain later said that during these carefree days, he had met every type of person on Earth.

The **Civil War** halted trade, so Clemens joined the **Confederate Army**. Two weeks later, he "resigned," his euphemism for desertion, and rambled westward. His prospecting and mining attempts failed, but the tall tales he wrote for newspapers were so convincing that they were often reprinted as fact. In February 1863, Mark Twain was born. The name is a riverboat term for "two fathoms deep," meaning that the water is just safe for sailing. Twain moved to California and based "The Celebrated Jumping Frog of Calaveras County" (1865) on a local myth. The story established his critical and popular fame.

For the rest of his 55-year literary career, Twain traveled and lectured extensively, and also penned several classics that were rooted in experience. In all of them, he combined his command of the English language and his unique humor with American vernacular.

*The Adventures of Tom Sawyer* (1876) centers around a mischievous but kind-hearted boy. Tom's hysterical and endearing exploits were partially based on the recol-

**Mark Twain.**

lections that Twain collected from his boyhood friends.

*The Adventures of Huckleberry Finn* (1884) is widely considered to be his best work. The story of Finn's trek down the Mississippi contains comedy mixed with cruelty and rough slang with poetic descriptions. The famous novelist **Ernest Hemingway** (see no. 85) would write that it was the first and best book in US literature.

Twain went bankrupt in the 1890s, and further charmed the public by paying back every cent. The deaths of his wife and two daughters, however, plunged him into a lonely depression from which he never recovered. Yet his witticisms, such as "Familiarity breeds contempt — and children," are still regarded as some of the finest ever uttered, and both Mark Twain and his extensive writings have become the subjects of numerous plays, television shows, and films.

# 57. GENERAL TOM THUMB
## 1838-1883

Thanks to the great showman **P. T. Barnum** (see no. 49), **General Tom Thumb** became the most well-known midget there has ever been. From his childhood tour to his extravagant wedding to his circus appearances, the nineteenth-century public could never get enough of this popular figure.

The son of parents of normal stature, **Charles Sherwood Stratton** was 25 inches (64 centimeters) tall and weighed 15 pounds (6. 8 kilograms) when Barnum discovered him. Taken to New York City, the five-year-old learned to dance, sing and tell jokes. Barnum then had several military uniforms made for the precocious boy and ballyhooed him as General Tom Thumb, an 11-year-old from England.

The general was an instant hit, and quickly became Barnum's most lucrative act. Well-attended performances at Barnum's just-opened museum were followed two years later by a tour of New England and abroad. In Washington, DC, Thumb was received by President **Abraham Lincoln** (1809-1865). In England, the newspapers made him a celebrity and he was embraced by the aristocracy. The crowning achievement came when the general received a royal invitation to Buckingham Palace. There, before Queen **Victoria** (1819-1901), he danced a hornpipe and did his impersonation of **Napoleon**.

General Thumb next caused a huge sensation almost two decades later, when a romance developed between him and a fellow midget at the museum, the 24-inch **Lavinia Warren** (1841-1919). Barnum, the eternal capitalist, offered them $15,000 to delay their wedding for a month so that he could further publicize it, but the couple refused, saying, "No, not for $50,000!" On February 10, 1863, thousands of people flocked to the Grace Episcopal Church to watch the ceremony.

Tom Thumb eventually reached a full size of 40 inches (100 centimeters) tall, with a weight of 70 pounds (32 kilograms). In 1881, shortly before his death, the general who never fought a war traveled with **Barnum and Bailey**'s "**Greatest Show on Earth**."

**General Tom Thumb.**

This flamboyant and adventurous US Army officer led over 200 cavalrymen to their deaths at the **Battle of the Little Bighorn**, ("**Custer's Land Stand**") the biggest **Native American** military victory of the nineteenth century. This 1876 debacle ignited a controversy that still rages today. At the debate's very core is the true nature of the mustached man himself — was his fatal error his reliance on others, or did it stem from a reckless quest for eternal fame? If that is indeed the case, **George Armstrong Custer** got his legendary status, but it cost him his life.

After graduating last in the Class of 1861 from the **US Military Academy** at West Point, Custer joined the Union forces in the just-started **Civil War**. There he quickly distinguished himself as a fearless cavalry lieutenant, and was temporarily promoted to brigadier general in 1863 and major general in 1865. Custer's dazzling performances at many battles made him a Northern hero, but the brave "boy general" did make some enemies. These soldiers called him a "glory hunter" and claimed his arrogance far exceeded his abilities.

At the Civil War's close, Custer, now a lieutenant colonel, was assigned to the **Seventh Cavalry Regiment**. In early 1876, his troops were assigned to aid General **Alfred H. Terry**'s (1827-1890) expedition to relocate the **Sioux** and **Cheyenne** tribes to reservations. The Seventh Cavalry was sent to Montana Territory, to an area south where the Sioux were believed to be. Terry's forces were to join the others in two days. Custer found the encampment of **Sitting Bull** (1834-1890) along the Little Bighorn River, and believed that his 650 men could easily capture the Native Americans present. In fact, he greatly underestimated their numbers, and his attack was met by over 3,000 Native American warriors.

Custer had divided his troops into three groups. Captain **Frederick W. Benteen**'s forces would prevent the enemy from escaping from the south. Major **Marcus A. Reno**'s men would cross the river and make an assault, while Custer's would do the same from the north. Reno's troops fought but retreated, where they were joined by Benteen's group. Meanwhile, in a battle that may have lasted just an hour, every one of Custer's force was killed. The only survivor was a horse named **Comanche**, and the animal would receive special treatment for the rest of its life.

Such a massive defeat, falling on America's centennial, shocked the nation, and a scapegoat was sought. Some people called Reno a coward, destroying his military career. Terry was blamed for incorrectly numbering the enemy forces, and George Custer has been alternately labeled a tragic hero, a racist monster and a fool.

**General George Custer.**

# 59. JOHN HENRY
## c. 1840-1871

In about 1900, this **African-American**'s victory over the steam drill was anonymously turned into one of America's most famous ballads. Countless other songs and stories about **John Henry** subsequently appeared all over the nation and traveled to Jamaica, France and Germany. In each version, he dies shortly after the contest, making him a universal symbol of the workers' fruitless battle against the spreading wave of industrial machines.

As John Henry's renown spread, his legend grew more and more fantastic. For example, it is said that when the 44-pound baby was born, the earth shook and the Mississippi River ran 1,000 miles upstream. Towns in every Southern state claimed John Henry was their native son, and he has been "positively" identified as an outlaw, a one-armed man with a thumb-sized wrist, and even a white man. If an English professor, **Louis W. Chappell**, had not investigated every rumor, eventually writing *John Henry, A Folklore Study* (1933), the truth may have never been known.

John Henry.

Born in North Carolina, John Henry was in West Virginia in 1870, working as a steel driver on the construction of the **C. & O. Railroad's Big Bend Tunnel**. It required enormous strength to drive long rods of steel deep into the rock. Explosives placed inside the hole were ignited, clearing away huge hunks of stone. John Henry, who probably weighed 200 pounds and was six feet tall, was the best steel driver of them all. He sang, joked, and played the banjo as well as cards.

Then the newly invented steam drill was brought to the site and tested on one of the crews. John Henry, with an aversion mirrored by **Mike Fink**'s (see no. 41) supposed hatred for the stream boat, announced that he could sink more steel than the machine, and a competition was planned. Although

some tales claim it lasted for a full nine hours, it was only 35 minutes long. While a huge crowd watched, the strong man swung two twenty-pound hammers as the steam drill labored at his side. When it was over, John Henry had made two seven-foot-deep holes, and his opponent, one nine-foot-deep hole.

No one agrees on the cause of his death, but it most likely came soon after his triumph. The ballads say that John Henry either died from exhaustion when the duel ended or from a broken blood vessel that night. He might have remained working there, but was killed during a blast or by a piece of falling rock. Some eyewitnesses claimed that he was buried at the tunnel's east end. For years after the duel, workers and local residents reported hearing John Henry's hammers clanging on steel.

# SARAH BERNHARDT
1844-1923

On-stage, her beauty, grace and voice left her remembered as France's greatest actress of all time. Off-stage, **"the Divine Sarah,"** as **Oscar Wilde** (1854-1900) titled her, could be bad-tempered but never lacked for lovers, making her one of history's most unforgettable theater figures.

The illegitimate daughter of a famous Parisian courtesan, **Henriette Rosine Bernard** was raised in a convent. The frail and willful child aspired to be a nun, but at age 16, her mother's lover and the half brother of **Napoleon III**, the **Duke de Morny**, enrolled her at the Conservatoire, a government acting school. There Sarah Bernhardt was not considered unusually gifted, but in 1862, again thanks to the duke, she was accepted by a national theatre company, the **Comédie Française**. Her performances went practically unnoticed by the press, and the following year, her contract was cancelled after she slapped a senior actress in the face.

During a sojourn from the stage, Sarah was involved with **Henri**, Prince de Ligne, and bore a child. While under contract to the Odéon Theatre, she slowly became noticed. Critical acclaim came for her portrayal of a minstrel in *Le Passant* (The Passerby;1869), and Napoleon III (1808-1873) received a command performance.

Sarah triumphed again in the lead of **Victor Hugo**'s *Ruy Blas* (1838). Hugo (1802-1885), who would be a rumored lover along with **Edward VII** (1841-1910), called her voice "golden," while others dubbed it "silvery," like a flute. The red-haired woman's love affairs with famous men were never far from the public's mind, and she drew shock by saying things like, "It is by spending oneself that one becomes rich."

Back at the Comédie, Sarah enjoyed several successes, and in 1879, despite stage fright, she gained notoriety in London as well. She then formed a touring company and became an international superstar, visiting major cities throughout Continental Europe, the Americas, Canada and Australia. Several romantic vehicles were written for her, and she built the **Théâtre Sarah Bernhardt** in Paris in 1899. It opened with *Hamlet* (c. 1600), with her in the title role.

In 1905, Sarah injured her knee, and later the limb had to be amputated. She continued to drive herself mercilessly, touring in seated roles and visiting **World War I** soldiers on the front. Sarah also wrote an autobiography (1907), a novel (1920), and an acting manual (1923). Her legendary status is illustrated by several anecdotes, such as that she had had over 1,000 lovers and often slept in a rosewood coffin filled with their letters.

**Sarah Bernhardt.**

# BUFFALO BILL CODY
## 1846-1917

**William Cody** gained fame as an amazing scout and **Native American** fighter, and used that fame to build a legendary show business career. He is most notorious for spreading the romantic image of the cowboy frontier through **Buffalo Bill's Wild West Show**, a fantastic exhibition in which he established himself to be as brilliant a showman as **P. T. Barnum** (see no. 49). Today the city he founded in Wyoming still draws tourists with its many attractions and exhibits.

By age 17, Cody was a **Pony Express** "centaur," besting Native Americans and robbers and riding through floods, desert heat and blizzards. After serving with Kansas' Seventh Cavalry during the **Civil War**, the dashing blonde-locked man supposedly earned his name while hunting buffalo to feed railroad workers. Buffalo Bill was said to shoot a pistol in each hand and hold the reins in his mouth as he rode through the herds. He slaughtered 4,280 buffalo in eight months, and became known as the best buffalo hunter of the Great Plains.

Cody remembered all the vast areas he had traversed, and became the chief of scouts for the Fifth US Cavalry, participating in 16 Native American conflicts. His adventures were faithfully reported by newspapers, and in 1869, he became a dime novel hero. There would eventually be some 1,700 of these publications devoted to Buffalo Bill. The sharpshooter authored several autobiographies and dime novels, and eventually starred in the drama *Scouts of the Prairie* (1872). Although his acting needed work, audiences were thrilled to see Buffalo Bill in action. He also led Western hunting expeditions for prosperous Easterners and titled Europeans.

**Buffalo Bill Cody.**

Inflated by his success and recognizing a thirst for a taste of the frontier, "the Prince of the Prairies" organized his "dramatic-equestrian exposition of life on the plains" in 1883. Buffalo Bill's Wild West Show had trick shooting, many of today's rodeo attractions, and staged dramas. These included buffalo hunts and various "cowboy and Indian" conflicts, with Buffalo Bill often saving the day. Among its other celebrities were **Annie Oakley** (see no. 68), **Wild Bill Hickok** (see no. 54), **Sitting Bull** (1834-1890), and several cowboy idols.

The show's triumphant 1887 showing for Queen **Victoria**'s Jubilee brought European acclaim, and it triumphed again at the **Chicago World's Fair of 1893**. Over its 30 years of touring, Cody made a fortune, but he eventually lost it due to mismanagement. However, his frontier hero status endures. This was proven in 1989, when the US Army reissued Buffalo Bill's revoked **Medal of Honor**, casting aside its long-held tenet that scouts were civilians.

# 62. JESSE JAMES
## 1847-1882

Even before his murder by a "dirty little coward," **Jesse James** was alternately worshiped as a **Robin Hood** (see no. 15) figure and condemned as a cold-blooded murderer. Either way, America's most celebrated bandit created the standard for the outlaw legend, inspiring future generations of badmen and setting the stage for the Western film genre.

The handsome son of a Baptist minister, Jesse, like most of his native Missouri, sided with the South in the **Civil War**. The blue-eyed teen-ager was nearly beaten to death as he tried to protect the family farm from being ravaged by Union soldiers. Jesse then joined a Confederate guerrilla band. When the war ended, a general amnesty was offered to all of them. As his group was riding to surrender, Northern troops ambushed them, and Jesse barely managed to escape with his life.

In the bitter climate of **Reconstruction**, Jesse and his gang began heisting banks, later claiming that they "were driven to it" by Northern bankers and railroad companies. Their maiden robbery, and also the first American one during daylight, was in Liberty, Missouri in February 1866. In their early careers, Jesse and his brother **Frank** worked on the family farm when not hitting banks from Iowa to Alabama and Texas. Whenever they were suspected, indignant denials written to newspapers would be accepted at face value by avenging posses.

The widely hated **Pinkerton Detective Agency** was eventually hired to capture the band. In 1875, detectives threw a bomb into the James farmhouse, injuring Jesse's mother and killing his younger half-brother. The press berated the agency, and the badmen gained public sympathy.

The following year, dozens of Northfield, Minnesota residents fought back when the **James Gang** attempted to hit their bank. Gunfire bloodied the streets, and

**Jesse James.**

Jesse and Frank were the only members to elude capture and survive.

By this time, the James Gang was looting trains and stagecoaches. Even when they were famed throughout the land, most Missourians would swear to the James brother's innocence. Jesse reveled in his notoriety. He collected the dime novels devoted to him, often announced who he was during robberies, and once left behind his own press release.

After killing a train engineer, a tempting $10,000 reward was placed on Jesse's head. One of his gang shot him while he had his back turned to fix a picture on the wall. Jesse's 25 robberies and at least six murders were forgotten in the face of his heroic myth, which portrays him as a savior to the downtrodden. Many thought that he faked his death, and as late as the 1940s, people were claiming that they were the magnificent Jesse James.

**Wyatt Earp.**

**Wyatt Earp** remains the most illustrious "good guy" of the Old West, with stories, books, and numerous films recounting the controversial shootout at Tombstone's **O. K. Corral**. Due to skill or perhaps just luck, this unforgettable figure triumphed in countless bloody gun battles against drunken cowboys, ruthless outlaws, and quick-draw artists trying to best a lawman.

As a teenager, Wyatt Berry Stapp Earp became a deadly shot with his six-gun, with accuracy taking precedence over speed. He said he met **Wild Bill Hickok** (see no. 54) in Kansas City in 1871, and that the other lawman convinced him to become a buffalo hunter for the army and the railroads.

Earp, a frontier rarity because he did not drink or swear, served as the law in the Kansas towns of Ellsworth and Wichita before becoming deputy marshal of Dodge City, "the Gomorrah of the Plains." He installed a fragile peace, often making arrests with the butt of his gun, not its bullets. He also befriended **John Henry "Doc" Holliday**, a fearless and perpetually drunk dentist who accompanied Wyatt, **Morgan** and **Virgil Earp** to Tombstone, Arizona.

There the new marshal soon learned that a crooked sheriff protected the town's stagecoach-robbing and cattle-stealing badmen. He had several brushes with the **Clanton-McLowery (or McLaury) gang,** and its leader, **Isaac "Ike" Clanton**, drunkenly boasted that the Earps would die trying to arrest any of his band. Wyatt would later insist that the entire battle was simply "a street fight" against "those who believed they could shoot down the Earps."

At high noon on October 25, 1881, the three tall brothers and Doc Holliday strode to the O. K. Corral. The Earps wore long black coats and broad-rimmed black hats, with string ties at their necks. During the bloody gunfight, which probably lasted less than a minute, Ike Clanton begged Wyatt not to hurt him, and he was allowed to escape. The other badmen perished, and Wyatt was the only participant to emerge unharmed. A huge legend began forming the moment the battle ended, and whether the Earps were murderers or saviors is still open to debate.

Wyatt and Doc Holliday were arrested for murder, but the charges were dropped. The vengeful Ike Clanton led several ambushes that left Virgil crippled and Morgan dead. The loyal Doc Holliday died a few years later, with his shotgun on the bed next to him. Wyatt wandered the West for nearly a half-century, and his third wife **Josie** was supposedly the former mistress of Tombstone's corrupt sheriff. Before his death, Earp spoke hopefully of finding a "peaceful obscurity I haven't been able to get in life."

**Belle Starr** married, lived with and sheltered several notorious badmen, but she was also a cunning outlaw in her own right. Tales about the glamorous "**Bandit Queen**" portray her as using her refined exterior to her advantage, but most of them are believed to never have occurred.

A judge's daughter, **Myra Maybelle Shirley** was born in Missouri, but as a teenager her family moved to Texas. During the **Civil War**, her older brother joined the same Confederate guerrilla band as **Jesse James** (see no. 62), and she is credited with keeping them informed of the Union troop movements. When her brother was killed, the expert rider and markswoman fought with the band. After the first robbery of the **James Gang**, for several months Belle and **Cole Younger**, Jesse's cousin, hid out in an Oklahoma cabin. He rejoined the gang, and she eventually bore a daughter.

The horrified Shirleys are said to have confined Belle to an upstairs room, but she fled with **Jim Reed**, another guerrilla, and they were married on horseback. In 1869, they and two others tortured a California prospector to learn where he had stashed $30,000 of gold. After Reed died in a gunfight, she created a lucrative horse-and-cattle stealing ring with a **Native American** named **Blue Duck**.

During this period, Belle reportedly moved to a Texas town. For several weeks she acted the part of a lady, charming a bank cashier until he was about to propose. One evening she visited him while he was alone at work. He invited Belle behind the railing, and she produced a pistol and fled with $30,000.

In 1880, she married a **Cherokee** named **Sam Starr**. The union produced two children. Their eastern Oklahoma cabin became a well-known outlaw hideout, and Belle and Sam continued livestock rustling. They were arrested and imprisoned for six months in 1883, but returned to their old ways. The Starrs later appeared before "hanging" Judge **Isaac Parker** in Fort Smith, Arkansas, but they were acquitted for lack of evidence.

Sam, like her first husband, died in a brawl. Three years later, Belle was riding home when someone shot her off her horse. Her killer was rumored to be **Ed Watson**, a neighbor she was attempting to blackmail, or her son, also named **Ed**. Neither was ever prosecuted, and the unsolved murder forever enhanced Belle Starr's mystique.

**Belle Starr.**

**Calamity Jane** is the subject of so many colorful legends — from scouting for **George Custer** (see no. 58) to having a passionate affair with **Wild Bill Hickok** (see no. 54) — that what is known of the truth seems almost dull by comparison. Historians claim the rifle-slinging frontierswoman in men's clothes was an illiterate prostitute and a hopeless alcoholic, but none agree on how she got her illustrious nickname.

**Martha Jane Canary** was raised in various mining camps in Wyoming, Utah and Montana. She was orphaned at an early age, and dressed in buckskin suits and wide-brimmed hats, the equestrienne wandered the West, taking whatever work she could find, sometimes at military encampments.

Her nomenclature was possibly earned before she was 25. Martha Jane may have given to herself to warn men that to offend her was to invite calamity. One account says a captain gave it to her when she saved him from certain death in a **Native American** scuffle. Martha Jane also may have seemed to bring danger on herself, for example, by frequently smashing buggies. It could have alluded to her bedraggled appearance after a drinking bout, or it may refer to the lovers attributed to her that died violently. The nickname may have originated when she heroically nursed the sick during a smallpox epidemic. It is known that Martha Jane was extremely proud of it, loudly announcing who she was so that her fame spread.

She may have participated in a geological expedition to South Dakota's Black Hills, but been kicked out when her true gender was discovered. In the spring of 1876, Calamity Jane moved to Deadwood, South Dakota, where Wild Bill already lived. Following his death a few months later, dime novelists dubbed her "the White Devil of Yellowstone," and this is when the tall tales began, most of them at her own invention.

Many sources believe Wild Bill thought Calamity Jane to be an irritating lowlife, but they may have had a brief affair. This turned into a fabled 1870 marriage, with a child later given up for adoption. She was also falsely credited with cornering Hickok's killer with a cleaver after the murder.

Calamity Jane soon resumed her ramblings, selling a leaflet of her fictitious adventures. After a failed marriage, she toured with various Wild West shows, but was invariably fired for drunkenness. She returned to the Deadwood area, and her last request, which was granted, was to spend eternity at Wild Bill's side.

**Calamity Jane.**

Diamond Jim Brady.

**Diamond Jim Brady**'s amazing business skills were eclipsed by his grandiose and generous displays of wealth that were extensively documented in newspapers. The public both resented and respected the robust multimillionaire's extravagant habits, which included wearing a different set of gems each day and freely handing out $100 bills.

Born in New York City, **James Buchanan Brady**'s ascent to wealth was not unlike a **Horatio Alger** (see no. 55) novel. After working in menial jobs, he started building his fortune in 1879 by selling railroad cars and other train equipment. On the road, Brady preferred to play cards for diamonds, not money. Many of the stones in his "Number One set" were acquired in this way, and all of them would eventually be valued at two million dollars.

Wherever he went, Brady enhanced his collection at local pawn shops, always getting what he wanted at a low price. Over the years, his stones grew in number and size. Sales became easier to close on his own terms, as Brady used the gems to impress prospects. If someone thought the diamonds were fake, he wrote his name with them in large letters on glass windows, spreading his renown and earning himself his famous nickname.

Diamond Jim returned to his native city, where he helped found two railroad car companies. It was then that his social life and exorbitant expenditures became regular newspaper features. Brady got his dog a set of diamond eyeglasses and entertained his friends lavishly, never bothering to recoup the money he'd lent them. On nightly visits to Broadway theaters and ritzy nightclubs, he was always accompanied by beautiful women.

One of Diamond Jim's longtime companions was the equally flamboyant actress Lillian Russell (1861-1922). He presented her with a $10,000 bicycle, a tribute paralleled by **Cleopatra**'s famous toast to **Marc Antony** (see no. 6). The bicycle had mother-of-pearl handlebars, with diamonds, emeralds, rubies and sapphires adorning the spokes. Brady left most of his estate to **John Hopkins University** and what is now the New York Hospital — **Cornell Medical Center**.

Like his lifestyle, Diamond Jim's gluttonous appetite for food was legendary. A typical dinner, so it was said, consisted of two or three dozen oysters, six crabs and lobsters, two ducks, a sirloin steak, several servings of turtle soup and vegetables, and a dessert of pies, cakes, and a two-pound box of candy. Diamond Jim reputedly said that he always sat four inches away from the table, and when he felt his stomach touching its edge, he knew he'd eaten enough.

Like **Jesse James** (see no. 62), this left-handed desperado was famous during his lifetime and gave the frontier its aura of menace. **Billy the Kid** supposably killed 21 men by his 21st birthday, but for many, his image as a heroic avenger glosses over his merciless nature. The skinny buck-toothed outlaw's heritage is still debated, and so is whether or not he somehow survived his assassination and went on to perform in Wild West shows, living until 1950.

**William H. Bonney** is credited with killing his first victim, who insulted his mother, at age 12. Shortly after his mother's death in Silver City, New Mexico, the 15-year-old was arrested for theft. Rather than facing his strict stepfather, Billy left town to wander, probably leaving several dead men in his path.

The following year, as a bitter feud stormed between ranchers in Lincoln County, New Mexico, he began working as a cattle rustler for one of the contingents. When Billy met one of his employers' chief rivals, **John H. Tunstall**, the English gentleman so impressed him that he went to work for him, seeing him as a father figure. When Tunstall was killed in 1878, the Kid, as he was now called, swore revenge. His targets included several former friends as well as the sheriff.

Billy murdered at least two of these men, and then with five others, killed the sheriff and his deputy. Because these victims were shot through holes made in a wall, he was labeled a coward and lost several supporters. Then the new sheriff and about 40 gunslingers found the Kid and 14 of his followers barricaded inside a rancher's mansion. The gun-battle lasted five days, with several newsmen observing and writing exaggerated reports of the carnage.

Billy miraculously escaped, later reneging on a deal from the governor that offered

**Billy the Kid.**

an automatic pardon if he surrendered. One anecdote from this period concerns a Texan who had bragged that he would kill the infamous outlaw. The Kid pretended to admire his expensive gun, but turned the cylinder to three empty chambers. When the two had a shootout, the Texan perished.

Then **Pat Garrett**, an old friend, became sheriff of Lincoln County, and captured the Kid in December 1881. He was sentenced to hang "until you are dead, dead, dead!," to which he replied, "And you can go to hell, hell, hell!" Billy, however, escaped by killing his two jailers. Garrett soon after killed the outlaw in Fort Sumner, New Mexico. He claimed that Billy was facing him and armed, but the pretty woman the Kid was visiting accused him of gutlessly shooting Billy in the back. She placed a wooden cross on the Kid's original grave that read, *"Duerme bien, Querido"* ("Sleep well, beloved").

This markswoman's astonishing skill and fetching looks won her devoted fans worldwide and a top billing in **Buffalo Bill Cody's Wild West Show** (see no. 61). The life of "the Peerless Lady Wing-Shot" became the basis of the musical comedy *Annie Get Your Gun* (1946), which has songs composed by the renowned **Irving Berlin**. The show depicts **Annie Oakley** as a bold tomboy, but the five-foot woman is said to have been a quiet, prim teetotaler, doing needlepoint and reading the Bible in her spare time.

**Phoebe Ann Oakley Mozee** learned to fire a gun at age eight, and paid off the mortgage on her family's farm by shooting rabbit and quail. At 15, she defeated the acclaimed marksman and vaudeville performer **Frank Butler** in a Cincinnati, Ohio shooting contest. They fell in love and were married the following year.

The Butler and Oakley team appeared in various shows and circuses before joining Buffalo Bill's fabulous exhibition in 1885. The long-haired Cody nicknamed her "Little Missy," while the **Sioux** chief **Sitting Bull** (1834-1890) dubbed her "Little Sure Shot." Oakley's popularity quickly eclipsed that of her husband, so he became her manager.

In her act, Annie, dressed in a fringed skirt and a deerskin jacket, never failed to faultlessly execute several unparalleled feats. These included shooting the flames off of a moving wheel of candles and hitting a dime in midair from 90 feet (27 meters) away. A playing card tossed in the air would be riddled with holes by the time it hit the ground. Because it looked like a punch-marked complimentary ticket, a free pass was commonly called an "Annie Oakley." She could also hit the thin edge of a playing card or several glass balls thrown at once. When Buffalo Bill took his troupe abroad, Annie shot the tip of a cigarette from the mouth of the German Crown Prince **William** (later Emperor **William II**; 1888-1918).

In 1901, Annie was injured in a train crash and subsequently resigned from the show. One of her legends tells of how the accident caused her chestnut hair to turn white overnight. She later toured with a theatrical group and entertained and instructed **World War I** soldiers. Annie Oakley and her husband proved to be a truly inseparable pair, dying just 20 days apart.

**Annie Oakley.**

**THE ELEPHANT MAN**
1862-1890

Although he looked barely human and frightened most people, "**the Elephant Man**" had a gentle, endearing charm that touched those who knew him. Sir **Frederick Treves**, a London surgeon who saved him from being exhibited as a monster, wrote a widely read account of **Joseph Carey Merrick**'s short sad life, *The Elephant Man and Other Reminiscences* (1923). It was adapted into a successful Broadway play, *The Elephant Man* (1979), and the following year, a film of the same name further immortalized his lonely existence.

Born to a slightly crippled mother, young Joseph developed normally until age five, when overgrowths formed on his skin and bones. It is now believed that he suffered from a very rare hereditary disorder called **Proteus Syndrome**. Merrick's nose was a mass of flesh that resembled a trunk, while his head measured over three feet in circumference. A deformed jaw prevented facial expression and made his speech hard to understand. Merrick's right arm had a 12-inch wrist and a fish-like hand, and his legs were much the same, forcing him to walk with a cane.

Joseph was sent to a workhouse at age 17, but he soon escaped. One chilly, foggy evening, Treves was walking home when he saw a canvas flap hung between two buildings. In the faint gaslight, the words "Elephant Man - admission twopence" were barely legible. He entered the space, and a figure sat wrapped in a tarpaulin. What Treves saw beneath it made him gasp, but he spoke with the huddled figure. When the men who displayed Merrick returned, they explained that they had found him wandering the streets, and had decided he might be profitable. However, many customers fainted or fled upon seeing their terrifying dis-

play, so they were happy to sell Merrick to Treves for five pounds.

Treves gave Merrick a private suite of rooms at the **London Hospital**, and made sure nurses could stand his appearance before interacting with him. Full of gratitude that his hard life had turned around, he quickly befriended all those with whom he came in contact. Merrick spent hours clipping pictures from magazines, and his favorite was one of **Princess Alexandra** (1844-1925), who would become the queen of England when **Edward VII** (1841-1910) took the throne. Although Treves tried to dissuade her, she insisted on seeing the popular patient. The princess was perfectly calm when he hobbled over and kissed her hand, but as soon as the door closed behind her, she fainted. Merrick later accidentally suffocated in his sleep.

Much to the medical profession's dismay, in death he would make another mark on history. Because for a long time it was incorrectly believed that Joseph Merrick suffered from an extreme case of **neurofibromatosis**, it was popularly dubbed **Elephant Man Disease**.

**Joseph Carey Merrick**

# CASEY JONES
## c. 1863-1900

This American train engineer bravely sacrificed his life to save those of others. Although he may have been partially responsible the collision, **John Luther "Casey" Jones** averted a major catastrophe. His gutsy tale has become the basis for countless ballads, some written and performed as far away as Europe and South Africa.

Jones was born in southeastern Missouri, but his nickname derived from Cayce, Kentucky, the town he grew up in as railroads were springing up throughout the nation. Not too much more is known about him, and the many songs devoted to him have obscured where the **Illinois Central**'s Chicago and New Orleans Fast Mail, also known as the *Cannonball,* was going on that fateful April day. Some accounts say the mail train was headed westbound to San Francisco, California, while others claim its southbound destination from Memphis, Tennessee was Canton, Missouri.

According to the early ballads, intense rains over an extended period of time left the tracks "like the bed of a creek," making the mail run eight hours behind schedule. The *Cannonball* left Memphis 90 minutes late. Jones, who had replaced another engineer at the last minute, resolved to remedy the situation. He was running hot and hard, making good time until Vaughan, Mississippi, when two freights suddenly appeared, blocking the main track. Jones ordered his fireman, **Sim Webb**, to jump to safety, while he heroically remained at the throttle. When the wreckage was examined, his body was found with one hand still on the brakes. Had Jones not remained there to jam them, the crash would have been far more severe.

An African-American co-worker, **Wallace Saunders**, wrote the first song, most likely saving the entire incident from complete obscurity. It quickly became a part of the growing bed of railroad folklore that included the legend of **John Henry** (see no. 59). A vaudeville team, **T. Lawrence Seibert** and **Eddie Newton**, revised it into a Tin Pan Alley tune, "The Ballad of Casey Jones" (1909). They popularized it in their act, and from then on, the tragic event was the basis of other songs. It also inspired a play by **Robert Ardrey**, *Casey Jones* (1938).

**Casey Jones.**

# NELLIE BLY
## c. 1867-1922

In a day when most women toiled in the home or the factory, this dark-eyed journalist was a fervent crusader for social reforms and womens' rights. **Nellie Bly** won admiration and awe for both her startling exposés and her undercover methods of obtaining them. As star reporter for **Joseph Pulitzer**'s *New York World*, the daredevil adventuress gained international fame for beating the fictional record of **Jules Verne**'s *Around the World in 80 Days* (1873).

Born in a town named for her father, **Elizabeth Cochran** was mostly home-educated. Shunning marriage, she searched for a job but her delicate appearance made her unfit for even kitchen work. A scathing letter in support of women's rights to the *Pittsburgh Dispatch* earned the 18-year-old a $5-a-week position there. Cochran chose the title of a popular song for her pen name.

When she began penning opinionated articles for the series "Our Working Girls," factories began banning reporters from their premises. Undaunted, she got a job making copper cables and shocked Pittsburgh with vivid descriptions of the horrible working environment. This clandestine approach became Bly's much-imitated trademark.

In 1887, she moved to New York City, and again couldn't find a job. Finally, the *World* offered Bly a trial assignment: fake insanity in order to investigate an insane asylum. Her widely read reports on its cruel, unethical staff and inhumane conditions brought changes to the institution.

In November 1889, with much fanfare, Bly set out to circle the globe. She travelled at a breakneck pace by steamship, train, rickshaw and sampan. In San Francisco, the passengers on her ship faced a two-week quarantine because their health reports had been left in Japan. Bly threatened to swim to shore, and a tugboat transported her to a waiting train. Seventy-two days, six hours and 11 minutes after she left, she enjoyed a hero's welcome in Jersey City, New Jersey.

Bly wrote a best-selling account of her trip and maintained a column at the *World*. Covering the bloody **Pullman Strike** outside of Chicago, she was one of the few journalists to sympathize with the workers. In 1895, Bly married a wealthy industrialist, **Robert Seaman**. After his death, she took over his business, providing employees with health care and equal wages. A string of misfortunes left the company bankrupt, and Bly went to Austria for a much-needed rest. However, **World War I** broke out, leaving her stranded abroad. *The New York Evening Journal* hired Bly as a correspondent, making her the first woman to cover the battlefront. Once back in the states, Nellie Bly continued exposing corruption and aiding the oppressed until her death.

Nellie Bly.

Most people know her nick-name, but the unfortunate circumstances behind her immortality have been largely forgotten. **Mary Mallon** generated two of the most famous outbreaks of typhoid when the grim disease was at its most rampant. In all, this mysterious carrier, who was herself immune, infected over 50 people and caused three fatalities.

Believed to have migrated to America from northern Ireland, the blonde-haired and blue-eyed live-in cook worked for several prosperous families in the New York City area. The first epidemic occurred in **Oyster Bay**, Long Island around the turn of the century, in the mansion of a wealthy banker. Officials were at first perplexed: no food or water in the household was contaminat-

**Typhoid Mary.**

ed, and no one there was a carrier. However, a cook had quit after the first case appeared. Further investigation revealed that typhoid had infected eight families for whom she had worked. Mallon had never been suspected; in one house, she had received a $50 bonus for nursing the afflicted.

Finally traced as an employee in a Park Avenue home, she was asked to provide samples of her blood, feces and urine. Instead of complying, the strong-willed Mallon chased the official out with a carving fork. Two more such attempts failed, but finally, in March of 1907, four men managed to drag her into an ambulance. Tests were taken, and it was determined that Mallon was the first permanent carrier ever found in the United States.

By now Mallon had earned her famous title, and the Health Department put her in solitary confinement at Riverside Hospital on North Brother Island, off the Bronx

coast. **Typhoid Mary** refused to provide any details of her background or employment history. By 1910, public opinion had swung in her favor, and she was released on the condition that she never work as a cook again. But she adopted an alias and resumed her former trade.

When the **Sloane Hospital for Women** in New Jersey had an epidemic of 25 cases, the cook, "Mrs. Mary Brown," was teasingly called "Typhoid Mary" by the other staff. On a hunch, a doctor there called an official who had investigated the Oyster Bay outbreak. Mallon's handwriting was recognized, and in 1915 she was quarantined at North Brother Island.

This time, Mallon was treated better. She had a job in the laboratory, typhoid was never mentioned in her presence, and she was allowed to visit the city. Following Mallon's death, her small estate was widely publicized but never claimed.

# 73. **RASPUTIN**
## c. 1871-1916

This peasant was a favorite at the court of the ill-fated Russian royal family (see **Grand Duchess Anastasia**, no. 86) because of the beneficial effect he apparently had on the sickly crown prince. Like the Romans' treatment of **Cleopatra** (see no. 6), the mystic's enemies helped install the widely believed notion that **Rasputin** was a cunning charlatan and a sinister **Casanova** (see no. 34). As a result, "**the Holy Satyr**" is remembered most for using his mysterious powers and hypnotic stare to seduce hundreds of women.

**Grigori Yefimovich Novykh** acquired his surname early on, and its meaning is interpreted differently by scholars. Most claim it means "debauched," while others say that in Siberia, the name was as common as America's "Smith." The illiterate youth, who drank, brawled and womanized, underwent a religious transformation, briefly joining a monastery and making pilgrimages to Greece's Mount Athos and Israel's Jerusalem.

Peasants supported Rasputin financially, seeing him as a staret (holy man) who foretold the future and healed the sick. Back in his village, he held well-attended prayer services, much to the village priest's displeasure. Some followers probably had affairs with him, but there were most likely no orgies around bonfires while Rasputin intoned, "Sin, because it is only through sin can you become holy."

In 1903, Rasputin was well-received in St. Petersburg, then in the throes of a mysticism fad. The unkempt wanderer was eventually summoned by Czar **Nicholas II** (1868-1918) and Czarina **Alexandra** (1872-1918) when their hemophiliac son was quite ill. Rasputin either simply prayed beside the bed or else hypnotized the boy; regardless, his patient recovered. He cured **Alexi** (or **Alexis**) at least two more times, once reportedly from a distance. Some said the prince

**Rasputin.**

stopped bleeding as soon as Rasputin entered the room.

Alexandra became convinced that Rasputin was essential to the survival of both her son and the monarchy, and encouraged her husband to use the holy man's comb before serious meetings. Rasputin behaved like a saint around the royal family, but supposably otherwise abused his power. According to legend, he drank, swore, and bedded countless women, claiming that physical contact with him purified their souls.

Rasputin's influence grew after the Czar went to the **World War I** front, but both he and the Czarina were perceived as enemy agents, with the German born Alexandra cast into a **Marie Antoinette** mold (see no. 39). Aware of his unpopularity, he is said to have predicted that he would be dead by the start of 1917. Meanwhile, three conservatives were conspiring to kill "the Mad Monk," but this was no easy task. After being poisoned and shot, Rasputin drowned in the Neva River in late December.

This Italian tenor, whose lyrical voice has been described as "golden," "velvet," and "carnal," has become synonymous with great opera. During his 26-year-long career, **Enrico Caruso** reached a larger audience than any star before him by being one of the first musicians to record his voice on the gramophone. The amazing success of his more than 200 releases, many of which are still reproduced today, is considered by many to have changed the primitive record player from a fad into a household fixture.

Born into a poor family, Enrico Caruso sang in the church choir but did not start training formally until he was 18. His Naples debut was followed by a tour of Italy, during which time he quickly learned many new roles. Caruso's first great triumph, in the world premiere of *Fedora* (1898) in Milan, came only because the original actor had suddenly died. The great artist would later explain, "After that, the contracts descended on me like a big rainstorm."

Caruso appeared in Moscow, St. Petersburg and Buenos Aires, and then returned to Italy for engagements at renowned theaters. Because he got bad reviews in Naples, he never again sang there. After performing in London and Monte Carlo, Caruso made his American debut at New York City's **Metropolitan Opera** in 1903. In his 18 seasons there, he would be the tenor star on 17 opening nights and portray over 35 different roles in French and Italian operas.

Caruso began recording albums in 1902, and within a few years, he had become the highest paid singer in the world. A single appearance in Mexico City earned him $15,000. Caruso's last record contract guaranteed a minimum of $100,000 in annual royalties, while his silent movie roles in *My Cousin* (1918) and *A Splendid Romance* (1918) are said to have paid the same amount.

Caruso's generosity became legendary, and he supposedly sent monthly checks to hundreds of friends and relatives. In private the plump man was said to be pensive, but in public he was outgoing and amusing. Caruso's last public engagement was on Christmas Eve, 1920, and was also his 607th performance at "the Met." By then he was suffering from a chronic chest cold, and his voice, still passionate and rich, had deepened in timbre. Diagnosed with pleurisy (an inflammation of the lungs), the opera star returned to Italy. Enrico Caruso ironically died in Naples, the one city he felt did not appreciate his immense talent.

**Enrico Caruso.**

# 75. HARRY HOUDINI
## 1874-1926

Harry Houdini became the greatest escape artist of the twentieth century by combining brilliant showmanship and physical dexterity with simple but subtle solutions. Thousands of people around the world clamored to see the magician's awesome exploits, which were usually done out of the crowd's sight. Amazingly, Houdini never appeared to alter or even unlock whatever he was confined to, whether it was a bank vault, a bag sewn shut, or a padlocked milk-can filled with water. He also never failed to win the seemingly impossible challenges made by the police forces of America and abroad. Perhaps for this reason, books about him are prison favorites.

**Erich** (or **Ehrich**) **Weiss** (or **Erik Weisz**) was born in Hungary, but his family moved to New York City in 1882. While still quite young, he worked as a circus trapeze performer and in vaudeville shows before deciding to become a magician. The muscled young man with the kinky hair took his surname from a famed nineteenth-century French illusionist. He married **Wilhelmina Beatrice "Bessie" Rahner** in 1894, and she became his lifelong stage assistant.

By 1900, Houdini was gaining international fame for escaping from handcuffs, prison cells, ropes, shackles, and the water-filled **"Chinese Torture Cell."** He extricated himself from straightjackets while suspended upside down from skyscrapers and from locked, roped and weighted boxes that were thrown into the Mississippi, Mersey and Seine rivers. Once, on the day Houdini was to do this trick in Liverpool, policemen arrived at the docks and confiscated the box. Suddenly the spectators began running to a site about 50 yards away, where the feat was already underway. Houdini, suspecting this sort of trouble, had placed a double at the advertised spot.

Different stunts had different secrets behind them. Houdini owned a huge collection of lock picks, and if he was strip-searched beforehand, one was slipped to him by an accomplice in a hand-shake, or, it is reputed, by his wife in a kiss. The milk cans, boxes, and coffins had hidden escape routes that did not involve their locks and seals. If he freed himself in a short time, he supposably read a book behind the screen while letting the audience's suspense build.

From 1916 to 1923, Houdini starred in silent films, often reenacting his fabulous escapes. He also led a campaign to put phony mediums and mind readers out of business. *Miracle Mongers and Their Methods* (1920) and *A Magician Among the Spirits* (1924) were exposés of their deceptions. However, Houdini was not a total skeptic when it came to spiritualism, for he and Bessie vowed to try and communicate with each other after they were separated by death. Houdini died first, on Halloween 1926, from a seemingly minor stomach injury. Before his widow passed away nearly 20 years later, she admitted that the experiment hadn't worked.

**Harry Houdini.**

Ever since her execution, **Mata Hari** has been known as the ultimate female spy, one whose seductive charm reputedly caused the deaths of 50,000 Allied soldiers. As such, her tributes in popular culture are countless. However, because her papers have been sealed until 2017, the truth and the myth surrounding the dancer-turned-courtesan are hopelessly blurred. Apparently, she was hired to spy for both the Germans and the French, and her lack of expertise led to her demise.

**Mata Hari.**

Although she would claim to be a sacred temple dancer from India, **Margaretha Geertruida Zelle** was Dutch, but she was uncharacteristically dark-eyed, dark-haired, and dark-complected. She did live in Java though, from 1897 to 1902, with her military husband. When the marriage failed, Margaretha went to Paris, possibly with only a half-franc and a gun. She took on a new identity, Mata Hari, which means "eye of dawn" in Malayalam.

Her erotic dances quickly became a sensation of the **Belle Époque**, and she proudly smoked the cigarettes named for her. "**The Red Dancer**" toured Europe, acquiring many powerful and high-placed lovers on the way. As her popularity declined, many of them supported her financially.

Some writers assert that before **World War I**, Mata Hari attended a German espionage school. She was in Berlin when war was declared, and many allege that she rode through the streets with the police chief while a crowd cheered. Mata Hari later claimed that she accepted 20,000 francs from a German consul to spy because her furs had been seized, and she figured the country owed her.

In June 1916, she returned to Paris, and was immediately put under surveillance. Setting a trap, the head of French counterespionage, **Georges Ladoux**, suggested that she spy for France, getting paid upon delivery, and the aging paramour accepted. In Madrid, Mata Hari became the lover of a German military attache, and which of her services he paid her for is still debated.

The Germans then started transmitting messages about their agent H21, and the contents made it obvious that they were referring to Mata Hari. Many argue that the Germans, knowing that this particular code had been cracked, used it for misinformation, and that Ladoux was aware of this. But many precious resources had been expended on Mata Hari, and France was in the throes of **espionitis** (a state of hysteria concerning spies).

She was arrested in February 1917, shortly after returning to Paris. Her reputation for using sex to her advantage is such that it was said that Mata Hari received her arresters naked and attempted to bed them to beat the rap. In fact, she was dignified to the very end, refusing to be blindfolded and flashing a rare smile to the firing squad.

Some legends tell of Mata Hari surviving with a new lover's aid. She is also credited with having two illegitimate daughters who were fathered by Germany's Crown Prince and an Indonesian Sultan. The latter supposedly also became an unlucky spy, being caught and shot by the Russians during the Korean War.

# PANCHO VILLA
### c. 1878-1923

Even before **Pancho Villa**, also known as the **Centaur**, became a hero of the **Mexican Revolution**, he was already deified as a **Robin Hood** (see no. 15) figure in dime novels. The portly, pigeon-toed and bow-legged bandit, who was himself raised in poverty, was adored by peasants for sharing his ill-gotten gains. As the guerrilla leader of the **Division of the North**, however, Villa was remorseless for his crimes, some of which were specifically targeted against Americans. When he was assassinated, the Centaur was a retired millionaire, with a large estate, several cars, and a bevy of mistresses and bodyguards.

**Doreteo Arango** changed his name to **Francisco Villa** after killing a man for deceiving his sister. During his youth, the excellent rider and crack shot was the leader of a mountain bandit gang. When the revolution broke out in 1910, Pancho fought for **Francisco Madero** (1873-1913), the contender to the incumbent regime. His 500 troops conquered several northern towns, and **Emiliano Zapata**'s (c. 1877-1919) did the same in the south. In two years, Madero was president.

**Victoriano Huerta** (1854-1916), one of Madero's administrators, put Pancho in front of a firing squad, supposably for disobeying commands. Knowing that his idol Madero would never order this, he begged for his life as his men raced to get a pardon. When Huerta had Madero killed, the Centaur again united with other revolutionaries, and Huerta was overthrown.

The man who bragged "I hit the enemy with one terrific blow!" was briefly president, with the approval of US President **Woodrow Wilson** (1856-1924). But after being defeated by General **Álvaro Obregón** (1880-1928) in the 1915 **Battle of Celaya**, the Mexicans and Wilson favored Obregón's superior, **Venustiano Carranza** (1859-1920).

In revenge, **Villistas** killed 15 Americans in Santa Isabel and 18 more in Columbus, New Mexico. Wilson then sent General **John J. Pershing** (1860-1948) and his troops to capture Villa. Mexicans, including President Carranza, resented the intrusion; Pancho gained sympathy, and the unsuccessful expedition was cancelled. In 1920, President Obregón gave Villa some land near Parral and a retired general's pay.

He turned his grounds into an impressive ranch and built a school for his workers' children. Still hot-tempered, Villa nearly shot an American reporter who asked to see some lasso tricks. The plot to kill the Centaur was planned with Obregón's approval. On the fatal day, a peasant vendor aided the snipers by shouting "Viva Villa!" as his car approached. As he lay dying, the indefatigable Pancho Villa shot and killed one of his assassins.

**Pancho Villa.**

At the height of his prolific career, people nationwide eagerly tore through newspapers each morning to laugh at **Rube Goldberg**'s newest **cartoon**. The cigar-smoking, left-handed "dean of American cartoonists" is best remembered for his hilarious, long-winded inventions designed to tackle everyday chores. They mirrored the nation's growing obsession with gadgets, and any ridiculously complex scheme or device is often termed "a Rube Goldberg."

**Reuben Lucius Goldberg** grew up in San Francisco, and at his father's insistence, graduated from the University of California with an engineering degree. His work was first printed on the sports pages of San Francisco newspapers. New York City beckoned, however, and Rube — along with his zany oddballs — landed a column at the *Evening Mail* in 1907.

"The Inventions of Professor Lucifer Gorgonzola Butts," for which Goldberg gained lasting fame, were drawn from 1914 until 1964. The instruments sometimes required hours to complete a simple task, such as de-linting a suit, and their serious instructions further enhanced their humor.

In 1915, Rube's work became nationally syndicated, and his salary skyrocketed. He proved to be a master of his medium, spoofing social gatherings and political events as well as new technologies, from the radio to the revolving door. Goldberg parodied **Mark Twain**'s *Innocents Abroad* (1869, see no. 56) with accounts of his own European travels, *Boobs Abroad* (1913-1914, 1918). His mastery of the one-liner is evident in such titles as *It costs too much to live and you can't afford to die* (1916), and he also made the slang term "baloney" popular.

During the Roaring 20s, Rube and his wife entertained frequently at their impressive Manhattan town house and hobnobbed with **Charlie Chaplin** (1889-1977), **F. Scott Fitzgerald** (1896-1940), **Walt Disney** (see no. 88) and **Harry Houdini** (see no. 75). He called on **Herbert Hoover** (1874-1964) at the White House, as he would later do during the **Truman**, **Eisenhower**, **Kennedy**, **Johnson** and **Nixon** administrations.

American humor began to change during the **Great Depression**, however, and Goldberg's work fell into a slump. In 1938, he successfully made a transition to a new medium — the political cartoon. Rube's most noted one, "Peace Today" (1947) earned him a **Pulitzer Prize**. In 1964, he turned to sculpture, winning the National Cartoonists Societies' **Reuben Award**, which he had designed, for his efforts. But the achievement for which Rube Goldberg was most proud came in 1966, when his name was a term in the *Random House Dictionary*.

**Rube Goldberg.**

This British soldier and military strategist was already famous for his **World War I** adventures in the Middle East when his epic account of them, *The Seven Pillars of Wisdom* (1926), was first published. By this time, **T. E. Lawrence** had shunned the limelight, and, in an attempt to anonymously research more books, had joined British forces twice under different aliases. Shortly after his military discharge, the reclusive hero died following a motorcycle accident.

Sir **Thomas Chapman** adopted the "Lawrence" surname after fleeing Ireland with his children's governess. The couple's second son, **Thomas Edward Lawrence**, joined an archeological expedition on the upper Euphrates river in 1911. He later explored Northern Sinai, on the Turkish frontier, in a covert surveillance mission. By the time World War I broke out, he lived, spoke and dressed like an Arab.

Lieutenant Lawrence was first stationed in Cairo, but he then became a liaison officer with the forces of Prince **Faisal of Mecca** (1885-1933), who was revolting against the Turks. He obtained British aid for them, and also helped organize and lead guerrilla missions. These mainly involved bombing the Damascus-Medina railway, making the Turks unable to send reinforcements. During these campaigns, **Amir Dynamite**, as Lawrence was known, sustained 32 wounds. He participated in the important capture of the seaport Aqaba in Jordan, and thereafter coordinated his troops' movements with those of General **Edmund Allenby** (1861-1936). It is said that in a single day, Lawrence of Arabia, operating from a Rolls-Royce, blew up two bridges, seized two Turkish outposts, and defeated a Kurdish regiment.

In November 1917, the Turks captured and brutalized Lawrence, leaving him with permanent physical and emotional scars. He escaped, participated in the Jerusalem vic-

**Lawrence of Arabia.**

tory parade, and fought his way north to Damascus. Back in England, Lawrence refused an earldom and other honors. At the peace conference of 1919, he wore Arab robes and unsuccessfully lobbied for its people's independence. Deciding that the Allies betrayed them, he retreated from public life.

Lawrence returned to the Middle East as an advisor to **Winston Churchill** (1874-1965), and saw Faisal become the king of Iraq. He enlisted in the Royal Air Force (RAF) as **John Hume Ross**, but was dismissed after the press found out. Next, as **T. E. Shaw**, he became a Royal Tank Corps private in 1923, and also continued his writing. When he retired to his isolated cottage in Dorset, Lawrence of Arabia was vacillating between periods of hope and bouts of depression.

This dapper colonel is the Southern gentleman image behind one of the world's most successful fast food chains, and his "finger-lickin good" chicken is currently eaten by over six million people daily. His rags-to-riches life was a paragon of hard work, from his **Depression-era** invention of his secret recipe, to his tireless promotions that contributed to **Kentucky Fried Chicken's** startling growth.

**Harlan Sanders** began his culinary career at age six, following his father's death. Kicked out of the house by his stepfather, the 12-year-old embarked a string of often menial jobs, taking correspondence courses in his free time. Often hot-tempered, Sanders quickly realized that he was best-suited to work for himself. In 1929, he

**Colonel Harlan Sanders.**

opened a Corbin, Kentucky filling station that also fed weary travelers. From the start, Sanders was obsessed by cleanliness and good service, and these, combined with his amazing cooking, made the one-tabled restaurant a hit. It soon proved to be too small for his growing clientele, so he opened a cafe across the street.

Sanders received his honorary title from the Kentucky governor in 1935, and perfected his blend of seasonings four years later. He was concerned about the half-hour it took to prepare the chicken, and deep fat frying, a quicker method, was unacceptable to him. A few adjustments to the just invented pressure cooker created the solution, a process Kentucky Fried Chicken still uses today.

**The Sanders' Cafe** closed after a new interstate highway bypassed its site, and at age 66, the bearded and goateed Colonel went on the road to sell his recipe to restaurants. In his trademark white suit and black string tie, he cooked meals for the staffs, and if they liked it, the owners would pay him four cents (later five) for each of his meals ordered. To assure his recipe's secrecy, the spices were mailed to the establishments. By 1964, the Colonel had more than 600 franchises in the US and Canada, and was earning a yearly salary of $300,000.

That same year, Sanders sold Kentucky Fried Chicken (now known as **KFC**) for $2,000,000, but remained on the corporation's board of directors and became its trademark. He began traveling about 200,000 miles annually for public appearances, and also appeared on TV shows and in commercials. Now gone but hardly forgotten, the **Colonel Harlan Sanders Museum** in Louisville, Kentucky displays such mementos as his first pressure cooker, and his face is omnipresent in over 9,000 KFC locations around the globe.

# 81. BARON MANFRED VON RICHTHOFEN 1892-1918

**World War I** was the first time airplanes were widely used to wage battle, and people took special pride in their country's heroic aces (pilots who shoot down at least five enemy aircraft), seeing them as the daredevil knights of the skies. The top ace of the war was Germany's "**Red Baron**," who is credited with 80 victories or kills during his less than two years of flying. The notorious enemy of the Allies was killed in action, and accounts disagree about who shot him down. His most familiar tribute is from cartoonist **Charles M. Schultz**, who has portrayed his famous beagle **Snoopy** pretending to be the accomplished aviator as he sits on his doghouse in flying gear.

Hailing from an aristocratic family, **Baron Manfred von Richthofen**, like his father, pursued a military career. He joined the German cadet corps in 1912, and was a cavalry lieutenant when the war broke out. He led a group of lancers, first in Russia and then during the invasions of Belgium and France. When trench warfare ensued, Richthofen joined the infantry. Discontented there, he transferred to the German Imperial Air Service in 1915. Having learned to fly, Richthofen enlisted in the just-formed jagdstaffel (fighter squadron) led by ace **Oswald Boelcke**. In September 1916, he scored his first Allied kill above France's Somme River. He realized that he loved the thrill of an aerial fight and devoted himself to improving his expertise, rarely socializing with other officers in his free time. Because his Fokker Dr.I triplane was painted an eye-catching bright red, the young pilot quickly became known as the "The Red Baron" ("der rote freiherr") or "The Red Airman" ("der rote kampfflieger").

In January 1917, Richthofen was awarded the honorable "Blue Max" or "Pour la Mérite." Recognized as Germany's premier air fighter, he was made commander of his own squadron based at Douai, France. This was later enlarged to include Jagdgeschwader (Fighter Group) 1, known as "**Richthofen's Flying Circus**" because its planes were a whimsical scarlet.

In July 1917, he nearly died from a bullet wound in the head. The following April 21, Richthofen was shot down near Le Hamel, France during a "dogfight" with Canadian Captain **Roy Brown** flying for Britain's **Royal Air Force (RAF)**. Some chronicles claim his Fokker was hit by Australian ground fire, while others believe that it was the captain who bested the mighty baron.

**Baron Manfred von Richthofen.**

With the histrionics of an accomplished actor, this bad boy of baseball slugged his way into America's heart, and also popularized the sport immensely. "the Babe" was paid more than the president by 1930, and his 714 home runs remained the world record until 1974. "The Sultan of Swat" was an emblem of the nation at its most glorious, and in **World War II**, Japanese soldiers attacked US troops with the insult, "To hell with **Babe Ruth**!" For many years, his best-known turf, Yankee Stadium, was known as "The House that Ruth Built," and the right outfield, as "Ruthville."

**George Herman Ruth** was born into poverty and sent to live in a Catholic boys' home at age seven. In 1914, the "southpaw" (left-handed) pitcher was signed on with the International League's **Baltimore Orioles**. His teammates gave the tall black-haired youth his nickname, but he was sold to the **Boston Red Sox** at the season's end.

**Babe Ruth.**

By 1919, Ruth's 29 home runs, the highest in the league, had eclipsed his outstanding pitching. His position was moved to the outfield or first base so that he could definitely bat. His Boston fans were incensed when the **Yankees** bought Babe in 1920.

"The Bambino" quickly became the main attraction of the incredibly successful New York team. The crowd's eyes were glued to the flamboyant "King of Clout" whether he struck out, was walked, or hit a homer. A man died of excitement while watching him play, and attendance rates fell when the pigeon-toed player was absent from the line-up. Ruth was especially idolized by children, and he once dedicated a home run to a boy he had visited in the hospital.

The colorful star was hard to manage, fighting with players and officials while on the field, and drinking, womanizing, and gambling while off of it. Regardless, his popularity soared. "The Behemoth of Bust" sold his name to a candy bar and other products, appeared on the radio and in films, and wrote newspaper articles and books.

By the time of his 1935 retirement from the sport, Ruth had achieved a seemingly endless list of distinctions. These include: a lifetime batting average of .342, playing in 10 World Series and on eight All-Star Teams, and setting or tying 76 pitching and batting records. He was one of the first players to be inducted into the **Baseball Hall of Fame**, and just before his death, he watched a film rendition of his life, *The Babe Ruth Story (1948)*.

This quintessential bureaucrat transformed the **FBI (Federal Bureau of Investigation)** into the efficient organization that it is today. During his nearly 50 years of leadership, **J. Edgar Hoover** taught America that the FBI "always gets its man," and he modeled public opinion to fit his own.

However, the nation's fascination for him stems largely from revelations that came out after his death. Some concern the lifelong bachelor's personal life, while others portray Hoover as an obsessive power broker who maintained his control of the nation by maintaining secret files on private citizens, politicians and presidents.

A native of Washington, DC, John Edgar Hoover considered entering the ministry, but instead worked at the **Library of Congress** while attending night school. After passing the bar exam, he became a **Department of Justice** employee in 1917. There Hoover investigated Marxist, Communist, anarchist, and socialist activities, and the resulting "**Red Raids**" led to 446 deportations. His hatred for "pinkos" grew more extreme and more irrational as he aged.

Transferred to the FBI (then the Bureau of Investigation), Hoover was as disgusted by the corruption around him as he was by the crime on the streets. When President **Calvin Coolidge** (1872-1933) took office, the 29-year-old became the FBI director. Hoover toughened recruiting standards, and established fingerprint, forensics and ballistics divisions, as well as a training academy.

Feeling that the country was too sympathetic to the gangsters of the 1930s, Hoover, with the aid of Hollywood, created the image of the "**G-man**," who never failed to arrest **Public Enemy Number One**. Because his agents were eventually not allowed to speak to the press, the now-dapper director and the FBI became synonymous to the masses. In the 1940s, Hoover's

**J. Edgar Hoover.**

targets were Nazi and Japanese spies, and in the 1950s, it was the Communists again.

By the 1960s, politicians knew that if they criticized Hoover, their indiscretions could well appear on the front page. He intensely disliked President **John Kennedy** (1917-1963) and his attorney general brother **Robert** (1925-1968), as they ordered him to attack organized crime and civil rights violations. Many say Hoover ignored the latter directive because of his belief that activists like **Rev. Dr. Martin Luther King, Jr.** (1929-1968) were Communists. To keep his job, he allegedly tracked the Kennedy affairs with **Marilyn Monroe** (see no. 96).

On the other hand, President **Lyndon Johnson** (1908-1973) is said to have maintained his own grip on Washington by reading Hoover's files each night before bed, and the director was similarly close to President **Richard Nixon** (1913-1994).

Following his death, Hoover's intriguing collection of scandal was mysteriously destroyed.

Most clowns are jolly creatures, delighting crowds with their brightly colored outfits and enormous grins. **Emmett Kelly**, however, captured the public's heart with his melancholy hobo persona. Wearing a ragged suit with beard stubble and a sad expression painted onto his face, "**Weary Willie**" became "one of the world's leading creators of laughter" with his perpetually futile antics. He not only amused circus-goers, but appeared in several other entertainment mediums that reached larger audiences, making him the most celebrated clown of the 20th century.

Kelly went to Kansas City, Missouri in 1917 with dreams of becoming a professional cartoonist. After holding several odd jobs, he invented Willie while drawing for an advertising film company. The sorrowful character, in his own words, "always got the short end of the stick" but "never lost hope and just kept trying. "

Kelly quit the job and worked in several circuses as a trapeze artist and clown. To set himself apart, he began performing as Willie in 1931. He chased the fleeing spotlight with an old broom, or fruitlessly tried to crack peanuts with a sledgehammer. Often he would just stare at a spectator while nibbling on a cabbage leaf. His routines were a hit, and his popularity grew.

Before **World War II**, Kelly began taking his act to England, and viewers there included **Winston Churchill** (1874-1965) and several titled aristocrats. During the war, he showcased himself on Broadway and toured the country's nightclubs.

From 1942 to 1956, Kelly was one of the star attractions of the "**Greatest Show on Earth**" (see no. 49). In 1944, an outdoor tent caught fire in Hartford, Connecticut, a tragedy that would ultimately take 168 lives. A news photographer captured the baggy-suited and red-nosed clown heroically rushing a bucket of water to the scene.

Another famous portrait of Willie was printed in *Life* magazine in 1947, and the forlorn figure remains a popular subject with amateur painters. He appeared in **Cecil B. De Mille**'s film extravaganza, *The Greatest Show on Earth* (1952), and also on many TV commercials and shows. Emmett Kelly, the genius behind Weary Willie, was described as a solitary and serious man who devoted himself to improving his unforgettable hobo.

**Emmett Kelly as Weary Willie.**

# ERNEST HEMINGWAY
## 1899-1961

This American writer's sparse style has changed the face of literature forever, and in many ways, **Ernest Hemingway** can be seen as a 20th century **Mark Twain** (see no. 56). Most of his utterly masculine work was based on the rugged adventurer's sporting and wartime experiences around the world, and he truly lived —and died — as one of his ageless and often ill-fated heroes. His many novels and short stories extol his principles, known as "the Hemingway code," which are epitomized by the phrase "grace under pressure."

Ernest Miller Hemingway was a young Kansas City reporter when **World War I** broke out. Rejected from fighting due to an old eye injury, he became a **Red Cross** ambulance driver instead. While serving in Italy, he was wounded and then decorated for his bravery.

After the war, Hemingway settled in Paris as a foreign correspondent. Other US expatriates there, such as **Gertrude Stein** (1874-1976), **Ezra Pound** (1885-1972), and **F. Scott Fitzgerald** (1896-1940), aided his writing efforts. *The Sun Also Rises* (1926), a powerful tale of the shiftless post-war "lost generation," established his fame, with which he had a lifelong love/hate relationship. After writing *A Farewell to Arms* (1929), a tragedy of passion and war, Hemingway traveled extensively. He documented bullfights in Spain, his big-game hunts in Africa, and his deep-sea fishing in Florida. As a newsman, Hemingway covered the **Spanish Civil War**, the background of *For Whom the Bell Tolls* (1940). During **World War II**, he was ostensibly a reporter, but he actually fought and became recognized for his bravery in battle and extensive military knowledge.

In about 1945, Hemingway settled in Cuba. While visiting Africa, he was seriously injured in a plane crash and reportedly laughed at the overhasty obituaries. Hemingway's final book, *The Old Man and the Sea* (1952), is about a Cuban fisherman who struggles to catch an immense marlin, only to see it get devoured by sharks on his return voyage. Seen as a tribute to man's endurance, it earned him a 1953 **Pulitzer Prize** and helped him win the 1954 **Nobel Prize** for literature.

Driven from Cuba by the revolution, Hemingway and his fourth wife settled in Idaho. There he tried to resume his life and work as before, but he was physically weak and losing confidence in his writing abilities. While being hospitalized twice for anxiety and depression, he underwent electroshock treatments that damaged his memory, and he supposably confided to a friend, "It was a brilliant cure, but we lost the patient." Shortly afterwards, Ernest Hemingway committed suicide.

**Ernest Hemingway.**

# 86. GRAND DUCHESS ANASTASIA
## 1901-1918?

Tsar **Nicholas II** (1968-1918) was executed during the bloody **Russian Revolution**, and the fate of his youngest daughter, **Anastasia**, has become one of the greatest mysteries of the twentieth century. Following **World War I**, many women claimed to be the Grand Duchess, most with the ultimate goal of obtaining the royal fortune. All but one were quickly discredited, and her true identity has never been decisively proved one way or the other. The idea that the deposed teenager may have survived inspired a French play, *Anastasia* (1954). Two years later, her title role in an American film version won **Ingrid Bergman** an **Academy Award**.

In July 1918, the **Bolsheviks** were holding the imperial family in a house in Ekaterinburg (now Sverdlovsk). According to most accounts, the Romanovs, their doctor, and their servants were awakened in the middle of the night, taken to the cellar, and viciously murdered. Their bodies were burnt, dismembered, and abandoned in a mine shaft. While it was later found to contain several personal items and a finger, no bone fragments or teeth — the hardest part of a corpse to demolish — were ever discovered. For many years, rumors circulated that all or some of the Romanovs had lived.

In February 1920, a young woman attempted suicide in a Berlin canal. When she was saved, she refused to speak, and was soon taken to a mental institution. Two years later, she confessed that she was Anastasia, adding that a soldier had helped her escape the cellar. They had fled to Romania and had a son, who was put into an orphanage. The soldier had died in a street fight.

Relatives were divided as to whether the claimant was Anastasia. The tsarina's sister believed she was not, but an uncle, who knew the Grand Duchess better, had no doubts. The young woman remembered

**Anne Anderson.**

trivial incidents that had occurred when Anastasia was a child, and she similarly convinced the family doctor's daughter. Later, a private detective asserted that she was a Polish factory worker who had disappeared in 1920, but her so-called brother did not recognize her.

In 1938, the woman, who called herself **Anna Anderson**, attempted to claim the royal title and its riches, and the court case dragged on for 32 years before she lost it. It was said later that an Austrian, who convincingly testified to seeing all the Romanovs dead, had also offered Anna his services for a lofty price. By then, she had married an American history professor and was living in Charlottesville, Virginia. She had cryptically changed her original story, only saying "There was no massacre there. . . but I cannot tell the rest." Anna Anderson — and her secrets — died in 1984.

As an apple-cheeked young man, he led a squad of incorruptible agents, "the **Untouchables**," who crippled the operations of the colorful mobster **Al Capone** (1899-1947). The newspapers documented their every bust, but **Elliot Ness** died impoverished and largely forgotten, just months before his best-selling autobiography thrust him back into the public eye.

An incredibly popular TV series (1959-1963) and a well-received film (1987) followed, both called "The Untouchables." Both shunned historical accuracy, but made Ness an American hero. On the TV program, a humorless **Robert Stack**, as Ness, submachine-gunned such outlaw notables as **Ma Barker** and **Bugs Moran**. In the film, **Kevin Cosner**, as Ness, slugged it out with **Robert De Niro**, who played Capone. However, although they despised each other, the two never actually met.

**Elliot Ness.**

Born and raised in Chicago's south side, Elliot Ness became a **Justice Department Prohibition Agent**. Drying up the Windy City was no easy task: the scar-faced Capone accurately bragged, "I own the police." In 1929, the cool-headed Ness was chosen to head a special force to harass the underworld figure, while another squad investigated Capone's taxes.

Ness hand-picked nine men with spotless records and experience in wire-tapping, surveillance, and undercover work. To enter Capone's alcohol-producing plants before evidence was destroyed and workers fled, the Untouchables used a 10-ton flatbed truck to burst though the doors in seconds. In June 1931, Ness obtained grand jury indictments against Capone and 68 of his associates for over 5,000 separate offenses. However, he was ultimately prosecuted and imprisoned for his shady tax practices.

By the time of Capone's trial, the Untouchables had shrunk his liquor empire to just 20 percent of its former scope, and at least four attempts had been made on Ness' life. Once he had deliberately angered the criminal by having 45 of his confiscated vehicles driven past his headquarters on their way to a public auction.

Ness later became the public safety director of Cleveland, Ohio, a post he would hold until 1941. There he was greatly admired for ridding the city of gambling, gangsters, and inept and crooked cops. Ness' failure to catch his nemesis, an elusive serial killer called "the Mad Butcher," began a string of bad luck that he never overcame. He lost a 1947 bid for mayor, and several once-promising business ventures soured. In 1956, he settled in a sleepy Pennsylvania town, whose residents doubted his claims of having once been an important crime fighter.

**Walt Disney** is revered as the creator of **Mickey Mouse** and the guiding vision behind numerous celluloid classics. His namesake company is synonymous with the term "wholesome family entertainment," and its theme parks in America, France, and Japan are the most popular ones ever created.

**Walt Disney and Mickey Mouse.**

Walter Elias Disney started his artistic career in about 1911, when a barber began buying his drawings for his choice of 25 cents or a haircut. He became a commercial artist in 1923, but barely stayed afloat. He is said to have invented the best-known Disney character on a long train ride, when he remembered a mouse who used to run across his drawing board. With *Steamboat Willie* (1928), the first Mickey Mouse cartoon with sound, both the mustached man and the zany mouse became world renowned. He presented the new character as his invention, ignoring the work done by animator **Ub Iwerks** who revitalized Walt's original sketch. Over the next 10 years, Mickey, along with other Disney characters **Minnie Mouse, Goofy, Pluto**, and **Donald Duck**, appeared in over 100 shorts.

Disney's first full length feature, *Snow White and the Seven Dwarves* (1937) was also the first full length cartoon feature ever. A resounding success, and it won a Best Picture Academy Award. His collaboration with **Leopold Stokowski** on *Fantasia* (1940) was considered an artistic masterpiece, although at the box office it was greatly overshadowed by other Disney Studios efforts such as *Pinocchio* (1940), *Dumbo* (1941) and *Bambi* (1942), which stand as classics of film anima-

tion. By the 1940s, however, many of Disney's staff had grown dissatisfied with their wages, and with his reluctance to give them credit for their work. Disney saw everyone as a happy family, viewing any insubordination as disloyalty.

A strike ensued in 1941, and the bad publicity hurt Disney Jdeeply. He took his revenge on the strike leaders, who were, ironically, some of his most talented artists. In testimony before the **House Un-American Activities Committee (HUAC),** he suggested that they were Communists, effectively damaging their careers. Disney reportedly made an agreement with **J. Edgar Hoover** (see no. 83), in which he became an **FBI** informant in exchange for the agency's investigations into his true parentage.

In the 1950s, Disney's studio produced a continuing series of classic animated features such as *Cinderella* (1950), *Alice in Wonderland* (1951), and *Peter Pan* (1953). The company also released several great live-action features, including *Treasure Island* (1950), *Davy Crockett: King of the Wild Frontier* (1955), *The Incredible Journey* (1963), and *Mary Poppins* (1965).

Walt Disney also originated the now-much-copied concept of theme parks. **Disneyland**, in Anaheim, California, was opened in 1955, and **Disneyworld**, in Orlando, Florida, being planned at the time of his death, opened in 1971. Today every addition to the magical world of Disney is an immortal tribute to its brilliant, though troubled, founder.

These two fearless pioneers embodied the restless spirit of the early age of aviation. By making the first *solo* transatlantic flight, **Charles Lindbergh** became an instant hero of mammoth proportions. **Amelia Earhart** materialized in his wake, and opened up the exciting but dangerous field to women. When Lindbergh's son was kidnapped, America saw a vulnerable side to their demi-god, and mourned alongside him. When Amelia Earhart disappeared, she became a bona fide mystery, paralleled by **Anastasia** (see no. 86) and **Kaspar Hauser** (see no. 50).

On May 20-21, 1927, Charles Augustus Lindbergh flew from New York to Paris in his Ryan monoplane, *The Spirit of St. Louis.* The Air Mail Service Captain and barnstormer not only won $25,000, but received numerous accolades and was compared to **George Washington** and the Biblical **Elijah**.

The next year, Amelia Mary Earhart became the first woman passenger to cross the Atlantic. Dubbed "**Lady Lindy**" because she resembled the pioneer, she too was transformed into a world celebrity overnight. As her piloting career began to skyrocket, she married the publisher **George Putnam**, who continuously kept her name in the newspapers. AE, as she called herself, made history on the fifth anniversary of Lindbergh's flight by being the first woman to cross the Atlantic solo. The much-awarded adventuress continued to set records and establish flying firsts.

In 1937, Earhart and her navigator, **Fred Noonan**, attempted to fly around the globe, but they and their Lockheed Electra vanished forever in the central Pacific. A massive air and sea search was fruitless. It was argued that she had been on a spy mission to investigate Japanese military installations, and that she pretended to get lost so that the military could also surveil the area. Or the plane had crashed and she and Noonan had been executed in Saipan. One fanciful report even had her living under an alias in New Jersey!

Meanwhile, Lindbergh had made goodwill visits to many countries and also pioneered various commercial routes. Following the celebrated kidnapping and death of his son, he took refuge in Europe. Upon his return, the man who had been decorated by the German military made several controversial speeches advocating neutrality in the growing conflict. Regardless, he managed to aid the war effort in the Pacific theater. Later, *The Spirit of St. Louis* (1953) earned him a **Pulitzer Prize**, and President **Dwight D. Eisenhower** (1890-1969) made him a brigadier general. "The Lone Eagle," however, disdained the limelight, explaining, "it's not what it's cracked up to be."

Charles Lindbergh and Amelia Earhart.

When this Swedish actress began starring in American films, she became world-renowned for her breath-taking looks and air of mystery and glamour. Her allure only grew following her reclusive retirement, which **Greta Garbo** aloofly explained with the famous quote "I want to be alone."

As a teenager, **Greta Lovisa Gustafsson** dreamed of acting professionally, but out of necessity, she worked as a department store clerk. There she happened to meet a film director, who gave her a small role and helped her win a scholarship to Stockholm's **Royal Dramatic Theatre Academy**. In the course of her studies, Greta met the prominent director **Mauritz Stiller**. He took her under his wing, costarring her in *The Atonement of Gösta Berling* (1924) and giving Garbo her celebrated name. When **MGM** offered him a contract, he insisted that the woman with the blue-violet eyes be given one too, as she was "an actress who will be the greatest in the world."

After her successful US debut in *The Torrent* (1926), Garbo starred in 24 more movies, playing opposite such swashbuckling matinee idols as **Clark Gable** and **Robert Montgomery**. It is a credit to her talents that she was able to adapt to the "talkies," something many performers were unable to do. Advertising for *Anna Christie* (1930) teasingly promised that "Garbo talks." The critics and the public alike were enchanted by her husky, accented voice, and their adulation grew.

Garbo contributed her mystique to an already exist-ing legend in *Mata Hari* (1931; see no. 76), as she had earlier done for **Sarah Bernhardt** (see no. 60) in *The Divine Woman* (1927). Her other notable films include *Grand Hotel* (1932), *Queen Christina* (1933), *Anna Karenina* (1935), *Camille* (1937), and *Ninotchka* (1939). The latter, a satire on Bolshevism, was followed by another comedy, *Two-Faced Woman* (1941). It bombed and, at 36, she left the silver screen forever.

The more Garbo attempted to live a private life, occasionally using an alias, the more the American and European press strove to cover her every movement. Her millions of fans hoped that she would return to the cinema, but she turned down all film offers. Garbo received a special **Oscar** for her movie achievements in 1956. She lived the rest of her life as a solitary New Yorker.

**Greta Garbo.**

# HOWARD HUGHES
## 1905-1976

The many accomplishments of **Howard Hughes** — as a film producer, aviation pioneer, and all-around business genius — have been largely forgotten due to his almost complete seclusion later in life. Whispers about his quirky habits, from a reputed obsession with cleanliness, to a supposed penchant for nudity and drugs, transformed him into a mystifying figure. Public fascination for the eccentric billionaire was so tremendous that a writer was able to sell the magnate's memoirs, which he had faked, for a reported one million dollars.

Following his father's death in 1924, Howard Robard Hughes took over the **Hughes Tool Company**. The company and its patent on an important drill bit were the foundation of his fortune. Two years later, the young man who resembled **Gary Cooper** became a Hollywood producer. He divorced **Ella Rice** in 1929 and was later married to "the starlet" **Jean Peters** from 1957-1971. His smash hits were *Hell's Angels* (1930), which was the first major role of the screen legend **Jean Harlow**, and *Scarface* (1932), one of the first gangster movies. Later, *The Outlaw* (1941) was based on the life of **Billy the Kid** (see no. 67) and starred the then-unknown **Jane Russell**.

He next founded the **Hughes Aircraft Company**, which became an important US defense contractor. Turning his seemingly endless energy to piloting, Hughes set many world aircraft speed and distance records. These included one for circling the globe in 1938. When he had to make a speech upon his return, he admitted that he was more nervous about that than he had been about his daring feat.

In the 1950s, Hughes continued building his empire. Once he saw something he wanted, whether it was a Las Vegas casino, or a company, he usually got it. By the 1960s, however, he'd become a bed-ridden recluse obsessed with germs. While negotiating deals, it is said that his right-hand man would hide under the bed. Using a code of pokes, he would tell Hughes whether the deal was advantageous or not.

Meanwhile, Hughes' fixation on privacy had captured the nation's curiosity. He would show up at luxury hotels in exotic locales with a small group of aides and bodyguards, who would ensure his total isolation by covering the suite's windows with black curtains. **Clifford Irving** created a massive scandal in 1971 with his forged "autobiography," which he said had been dictated to him by the man himself. Hughes denied this, and Irving was eventually jailed.

After his death while flying to Texas for medical care, several so-called wills making claims on his two billion dollar estate were rejected by the courts. Those close to the elusive entrepreneur assert that he never made one, not wanting to acknowledge his own mortality.

**Howard Hughes as a young pilot.**

This criminal couple has an aura of romance, thanks to a popular 1967 film that starred **Warren Beatty** and **Faye Dunaway** and misrepresented the two as well-loved **Robin Hood** (see no. 15) figures. The real **Bonnie and Clyde** blamed the **Great Depression** for their unlawful deeds as **Jesse James** (see no. 62) had similarly faulted **Reconstruction**, but unlike him, they never had any popular support while they preyed on the Southwest.

Bonnie and Clyde were instead widely perceived as heartless degenerates who enjoyed taking lives, especially those of police officers. Most newspapers of the day portrayed them in this vein, and the notorious gangster **John Dillinger** called them "snot-nosed punks" who were "giving bank robbing a bad name." Regardless of their true natures, Bonnie and Clyde's exploits caused a souvenir-hunting crowd to descend on their bloodied Ford within moments of their deaths.

In January 1930, Clyde Champion Barrow and Bonnie Parker fell in love at first sight. During their courtship, the petite blonde became an expert markswoman. The Texans began their robbery career soon after, with Bonnie often driving the getaway car while Clyde, on the running board, imitated old-time gunslingers by shooting up the town.

Clyde was arrested shortly thereafter, but escaped after Bonnie slipped him a .38 revolver that was taped to her thigh. He was eventually caught and rejailed, not getting released until February 1932. In late March, Bonnie was captured while Clyde fled the scene of stolen car chase. Three months later, she returned to the ever-changing ranks of the Barrow gang.

Over the next two years, there were several disappointing bank hauls and countless lucky escapes from the law. Occasionally they kidnapped cops and eventually released them unharmed. However at least 10 other officers and store owners were not so fortunate.

Several snapshots of the joking twosome that were recovered from a safe house were published worldwide. Bonnie especially reveled in their bad-guy image, and her poem, "The Story of Bonnie and Clyde" recognized that they would die in a shoot-out. Then one former member, perhaps trying to avoid the electric chair, alleged that he was forced to stay in the gang by a perverted Bonnie and Clyde, a characterization of them that has been accepted by most historians.

In exchange for a pardon, another gang member arranged to meet them on a Louisiana road, where a posse was also waiting. Clyde was shoeless and Bonnie was eating a sandwich when they were surprised by a barrage of bullets, which in four minutes left 167 holes in their stolen car.

**Clyde Barrow and Bonnie Parker.**

At the height of his fame, he was America's number one cowboy hero, and she was his leading lady. Together, they starred in 35 low-budget Westerns, as well as in the much-loved "**Roy Rogers Show**" (1951-1964). Wearing his white trademark ten-gallon hat, **Roy Rogers** never failed to best the bad guys, and usually crooned a bit along the way.

Born in Ohio, **Leonard Franklin Slye** learned to sing and play guitar at a young age. After working on farms in California, he performed with several bands and began appearing on the radio and in films. His big break came when **Gene Autry** backed out of his latest vehicle due to a contract dispute.

For this movie, called *Under Western Stars* (1938), the newly named Roy Rogers had his choice of several stallions. He picked **Trigger**, "the smartest horse in the movies." Believing that "any cowboy worth his stuff owes half of what he gets to his horse," he gave his palomino second billing, in front of his humorous sidekick, **George "Gabby" Hayes**, as well as the green-eyed singer **Dale Evans** (nee **Frances Octavia Smith**), who started working with him astride her horse **Buttercup** in 1944. Although "the Queen of the West" and "the King of the Cowboys" married three years later, they never kissed on-screen.

Meanwhile, Rogers had become a full-blown superstar. He received a record 75,000 fan letters in one month, there were over 2,000 fan clubs in the US, and the London chapter had 50,000 members. Roy Rogers merchandise deluged stores, and he and Trigger added their hand-, foot- and hoof-prints to the famous **Grauman's Chinese Theatre** in Hollywood.

During the TV show's run, Rogers continued to appear in films, which eventually numbered 91. He and Evans, who by now had her own toy and clothing lines, toured with rodeos, played at state fairs, and released several albums. Both are devout Christians, and Dale's book, *Angel Unaware* (1953), is an uplifting chronicle of their daughter's life and untimely death. The couple also raised the children from their first marriages and adopted several others, but still found the time to entertain US troops in Vietnam.

Today, the **Roy Rogers-Dale Evans Museum** in Victorville, California contains many mementos from their careers. Roy Rogers also established a chain of fast-food restaurants that bear his name. As an old friend of the actor-turned-president **Ronald Reagan** (b. 1911), he was once asked by the Republicans to run for Congress. The cowboy rejected them, saying, "I don't want to get involved in things I don't know much about."

**Roy Rogers and Dale Evans.**

Long after her death, **Evita**, the beautiful blonde wife of Argentine president **Juan Perón** (1895-1974), continued to be idolized as a selfless champion of the working-class masses. However, her enemies persisted in castigating her as a greedy prostitute. Eva Perón was as paradoxical as her legacy, for she kissed lepers but wore expensive designer clothes from Paris. The most prominent and flattering tribute to "the Bridge of Love" is the musical *Evita* (1978).

**María Eva Duarte** was illegitimate, a stigma she tried to hide her entire life. At 15, she went to Buenos Aires and became a radio and film actress, and her detractors claim that she built her fame on promiscuity. In 1944, Eva met Colonel Perón, then the Secretary of Labor, and became his first and biggest supporter. When the military government arrested him, she successfully rallied his followers, known as the decamisados, or shirtless ones, to march for his release.

The couple married and Perón became president in 1946. Evita was the unofficial liaison with the unions, who would remain staunchly loyal to them. Following the institution of women's suffrage, "the South American Eleanor Roosevelt" started the **Perónist Women's Party**. Her next project, the **Eva Perón Foundation**, built hospitals, schools, and orphanages throughout the country, and its founder personally met with and aided families every day.

While Evita always treated the poor with respect, she is often characterized as being arrogant and rude to others. She was also a workaholic: during one vacation, Perón had the phone disconnected, but she had it hooked back up, and hid it under a cushion to muffle its ring.

Evita was to run for vice-president in 1951, but this was blocked by the military. At a huge political rally, "the Lady of Hope," already sick with cancer, stated that she would not seek political office. This

**Eva Perón**

noble "renunciation," as it became known, only boosted her hold over the people, and she was officially titled "the Spiritual Leader of the Nation."

Her death, coming at the height of her popularity, was seen as a result of her untiring devotion to Argentina. She was made a candidate for canonization, and the lines to view her in state stretched for 30 blocks. After Perón's 1955 exile, Evita's embalmed body was hidden in Italy by the new government, who feared that she threatened their power. She next became a revolutionary icon, and her corpse was returned to Perón, who soon became president again.

His successor and next wife, **Isabel**, put Evita's remains in a crypt in the Presidential Palace, along with those of Perón. When she was ousted from office, the cadaver was finally interred in her family's tomb, which is said to be burglar-proof and able to withstand a nuclear bomb.

**Audie Murphy**'samazing single-handed feat gave him the fame of a real-life Rambo. He received 24 medals from his country as well as three from France and one from Belgium, making him the most decorated American soldier of **World War II**. Of the seven medals for heroism that can be awarded, five were given to Murphy. The boyish-looking idol later acted in several Hollywood films, becoming even more of a public fixture.

At 18, Audie Leon Murphy supposably had to beg his way into the Army infantry. It is said that later, the short Texan had to do the same thing in order to get an assignment abroad. Murphy consistently fought valiantly, and he was promoted to second lieutenant in 1944.

On January 26, 1945, near Colmar, France, Murphy's unit was greatly outnumbered by German troops, and he ordered his men to retreat while he remained at the front. Via telephone, he gave the artillery specific locations to bomb, many of which were dangerously close to himself. Meanwhile, he fought with whatever weapons he came across. Murphy mounted a burning tank destroyer and fired its machine gun whenever the air cleared enough to aim at the storming troops. When the enemy realized where the bullets were coming from, they were afraid to shoot at him, as that could have possibly set off an explosion.

He ordered a direct blast to the vehicle, and then jumped to safety at the last possible moment. The lieutenant then killed the remaining German troops, leaving, by one estimate, 240 dead.

**Audie Murphy.**

Murphy was given many awards and tributes, including the much-coveted **Congressional Medal of Honor**, the United States' premier medal for heroism under fire, given for "bravery or self-sacrifice above and beyond the call of duty."

Shortly after this, in 1948, he started his motion picture career. Murphy starred in *The Red Badge of Courage* (1951), an adaptation of the **Stephen Crane** novel, and *To Hell and Back* (1955), a dramatization of his own adventures. He also appeared in *The Quiet American* (1957), a tale that takes place in war-torn Saigon. Murphy's other movie work mostly consisted of low-budget Westerns. The courageous lieutenant was killed in a tragic airplane crash near Roanoke, Virginia.

Marilyn Monroe was a dynamic vision of innocence and eroticism, adulated around the globe. A devastating personal life culminated in her mysterious death at 36, and the scandalous questions it raised contribute to the eternal mystique of Hollywood's premier sex goddess.

Norma Jean Mortenson (or Baker) spent much of her childhood in orphanages and foster homes, the conditions of which she would later exaggerate to the press. She married at 16, but left her husband to pursue her Hollywood dreams. During her first years there, Marilyn often got bit parts via the proverbial casting couch. In 1952, she was propelled to stardom when the press found out that she had posed nude while struggling to survive. One of these much-reproduced shots later graced the inaugural cover and centerfold of Playboy.

Every film the quintessential "dumb blonde" made, from *The Seven Year Itch* (1955), to *Some Like It Hot* (1959), was a box-office smash. Off-screen, the insecure Marilyn had perpetual stage fright, and once 65 takes were needed for a three-word line. Her stormy marriage to baseball legend Joe DiMaggio (b. 1914) ended in divorce, and she left Hollywood, enrolling in the prestigious Actors Studio. Marilyn next wed playwright Arthur Miller (b. 1915), but this union dissolved after production of her final film, *The Misfits* (1961), which Miller had written for her.

The busty sex symbol, whose possible affairs included Marlon Brando (b. 1924), Howard Hughes (see no. 91), and popular

**Marilyn Monroe.**

singer Frank Sinatra (b. 1915), reputedly began a love affair with President John F. Kennedy (1917- 1963). However, Marilyn was meanwhile said to be deeply in love with his brother, Attorney General Robert "Bobby" Kennedy (1925-1968). After the studio suspended her for lateness and absenteeism, she supposedly tried to convince him to leave his wife and marry her. When he rejected her, she may have planned to go public with the Kennedy indiscretions.

If that is so, Marilyn died first, and after an investigation plagued by unanswered questions, her death was ruled to have been a suicide, although it may have been an accidental overdose.

This seemed overtly plausible, as for years she had self-destructively vented her depression over issues such as her childlessness into heavy prescription drug usage.

Yet the debate over her death continues. Many believe her fatal dose was administered at the behest of organized crime or sinister forces within the government. Organized crime motives would have been to indebt the Kennedys to them, as the brothers endangered their empires. One of FBI chief J. Edgar Hoover's (see no. 83) missing files allegedly concerns the matter. The truth will probably never be known.

The world was shocked by Marilyn's death, and the interest in her and love for her has not abated. For 20 years, the grief-stricken DiMaggio had red roses delivered to her crypt three times a week, and Marilyn still intrigues and enchants the masses.

Grace Kelly is still regarded as the epitome of sophisticated beauty, and her charmed life seemed like one of her movie scripts — especially when she abandoned her career at its peak to marry the prince of Monaco. This fairy tale perfection was shattered by her tragic death, which only enlarged her timeless myth.

At 18, the Philadelphia debutante went to New York City to study acting, and then became a model and appeared in TV commercials. Grace's theater debut was in a revival of *The Torchbearers* (1922), which was written by her acclaimed playwright uncle, **George Kelly** (1887-1974). Her first **Broadway** performance came the same year, in *The Father* (1949).

After a bit role in the movie *Fourteen Hours* (1951), Grace went to Hollywood. There her cool blonde looks earned her several impressive roles. Grace played **Gary Cooper**'s wife in the Western classic *High Noon* (1952), and opposite **Clark Gable** in *Mogambo* (1953). She also won an **Academy Award** for best actress for her portrayal of a frumpy wife in *The Country Girl* (1954).

Grace found her ultimate niche in the nail-biting thrillers directed by cinema great **Alfred Hitchcock** (1899-1980). He was captivated by what he called her "sexual elegance," and she is regarded by many as the ultimate Hitchcock heroine. *Dial M for Murder* (1954) was followed by *The Rear Window* (1954) with **James Stewart**, arguably one of Hitchcock's finest masterpieces. **Cary Grant** was her love interest in *To Catch a Thief* (1955), but during its filming in France, she met her real-life Romeo, Prince **Rainier III** of Monaco (b. 1923), to whom she was married in 1956.

Grace returned to Hollywood to make *The Swan* (1956) and *High Society* (1956), but then embarked on what was perhaps her greatest role, that of the princess of Monaco. The storybook wedding made world headlines, but her fans were extremely sad to see her leave the big screen. With this in mind, "the Master of Suspense" envisioned *Marnie* (1964) with Grace in the lead, but she stayed in retirement, so the part went to **Tippi Hedren** instead.

As Princess Grace of Monaco, she devoted herself to her husband and three children, Caroline, Stephanie and Albert. Her fatal car accident occurred on the twisting roads of France's Côte D'Azur region, the same curves she and Cary Grant drove in her last Hitchcock film.

**Grace Kelly.**

# D.B. COOPER
## 19??-1971?

D.B. **Cooper** became a national hero by pulling off the first successful US hijacking and then completely disappearing. Law enforcement officials have never traced his identity, and whether or not he survived is still open to debate. At the height of his popularity, T-shirts bearing the slogan "D.B. COOPER — WHERE ARE YOU?" were commonplace, and his name was a household word. Since then, books, articles, and a film have been devoted to him, and the residents of Ariel, Washington hold an annual celebration in a tribute to him.

In Portland, Oregon on Thanksgiving Eve, November 24, 1971, a middle-aged man giving his name as **Dan Cooper** paid cash for a ticket on Northwest Orient's Flight 305 to Seattle, Washington. He was extremely ordinary-looking, with no distinguishing features that anyone could remember. He carried a case that was not examined, as this was before the days of airport security checks. After take off, Cooper handed the stewardess a note. It requested four parachutes and $200,000 in $20 bills; if these demands were not met, he would blow up the plane.

The captain thought this was a hoax until Cooper calmly opened his attaché, revealing sticks of dynamite connected to a battery by a mass of wires. The captain relayed the skyjacker's demands to the authorities, who decided to cooperate. In Seattle, the parachutes and the money, which had been marked, were moved onto the craft, and the 32 passengers disembarked unharmed.

The airliner now headed for Reno, Nevada. Cooper instructed the captain not to exceed an altitude of 10,000 feet or a speed of 200 mph. Various Air Force and police aircraft followed the Boeing 727, but as the night was rainy and windy, it was hard to

D.B. Cooper.

keep it in sight. Inside, the crew members were ordered to stay in the cockpit, but due to a rocking motion they felt, they told agents that Cooper probably jumped out over the Lewis River in southwest Washington.

The press latched onto the story of the daring skyjacker, incorrectly calling him D.B. Cooper, and the name stuck. The police and the **FBI** believed that he had been killed in the fall, perhaps by drowning. However, their intensive searches of the area found nothing, and people began to feel that he had lived after all. In 1980, $5,800 of the cash was recovered in the Columbia River near Vancouver, Washington. The find was cryptic, though: had the loot washed downstream from the site of Cooper's death, or was it placed there to confuse his pursuers? There have been many intriguing solutions offered to this baffling case, which is the only unsolved skyjacking in America, but the fate of the elusive D.B. Cooper remains a mystery.

*In Rebel Without a Cause* (1955), **James Dean** emerged as the spellbinding symbol of the alienation experienced by the world's young generation. By that time, the incredibly expressive and handsome actor had already died in a car crash, and this earned him a spot in the pantheon of Hollywood stars tragically cut down and eternally frozen in their prime, a god-like realm **Marilyn Monroe** (see no. 96) later entered.

As a child, James Byron Dean's favorite game was inventing plays on a toy theater stage with his mother, who died when he was nine years old. After studying drama in California, Jimmy attended the famed **Actors Studio** in New York City. There he mastered its technique, called **the Method**, which requires a total immersion in the role. This expertise, along with his vulnerable, searching looks, assured his stardom.

Jimmy acted in several TV dramas, and then appeared in the **Broadway** plays *See the Jaguar* (1952) and **The Immoralist** (1954). The latter won him a **Tony award**, and enabled him to land a major part in *East of Eden* (1955), in which he portrayed a brooding son perpetually rejected by his father. During its production, Dean became seriously involved with the Italian starlet **Pier Angeli**. He considered joining the Catholic church and started wearing suits to please her conservative family, but she got engaged to someone else. Later Pier confessed, "He is the only man I ever loved . . . as a woman should love a man."

Dean next portrayed the cigarette-smoking, red-jacketed **Jim Stark** in *Rebel Without a Cause*, a tale of adolescent angst and delinquency. He improvised one of the movie's finest moments, in which he covers a monkey doll with a newspaper as he lies in the street drunk.

When its filming was completed, Jimmy went on location for the Texas melodrama *Giant* (1956), throwing himself into the frustrated **Jett Rink** character by acquiring a drawl and learning various cowboy skills.

Back in California, James Dean got into a fatal collision while driving his silver Porsche Spyder. Many of his countless fans know offhand that exact time he died, 5:59 pm on September 30, 1955. *Rebel* opened October 3rd, and the legend was born. **Warner Brothers** hesitantly released *Giant* the following year, fearing the reaction of Jimmy's mourners around the globe. His struggles on-screen echoed their own, and they felt his death as if they had lost a close friend.

Fascination with James Dean still endures. There was talk of a *Rebel* curse after co-stars **Natalie Wood** and **Sal Mineo** also came to dire ends. Acting careers have been made because of a resemblance to the cult hero, and he remains an emblem of youthful confusion.

**James Dean.**

**Elvis Presley** is the undisputed King of Rock of Roll, and his fame has snowballed since his death. Worldwide, fans idolize the music pioneer in their persona of choice — as the ultimate sex symbol, a messiah whose generosity knew no bounds, a **Horatio Alger** hero (see no. 55) with a Southern accent, or a mega-superstar who ruled Las Vegas in an appropriately Bacchanalian fashion.

Some zealots believe he is alive, and many have a special "Elvis room" for his mementos. Each year, over half a million people make pilgrimages to his famous landmark home, **Graceland**, a flashy mansion in Memphis, Tennessee. Impersonators come in all sizes and races, and often see themselves as "priests" carrying on the work of their absent god.

Born in Tupelo, Mississippi, Elvis Aron Presley was a truck driver when he made his first recording. Soon the boy who never had a music lesson was gyrating before hysterical and mostly female teenage crowds. By 1956, the charismatic and controversial "Elvis the Pelvis" was the first major rock star, releasing million-selling hits like "Heartbreak Hotel" and "Hound Dog."

Elvis was drafted in 1958, and he met his future wife, the 14-year-old **Priscilla Beaulieu**, in Germany. Her parents let her move to Memphis, and "the live-in Lolita" was molded into his mirror image. Elvis primarily associated with his entourage, "the Memphis Mafia," and he lived extravagantly, buying pricey accouterments and renting movie theaters or amusement parks nightly.

Throughout his career, the priority of his manager, **Andreas van Kuijk** — a fugitive illegal alien turned circus promoter who called himself Colonel **Tom Parker** — was to make a quick buck. He made many. One of the unfortunate results of the Colonel's vision of Elvis as an entertainer was his being sidetracked into the rut of a forgettable, campy movies. When his film contract ended in 1968, his popularity was diminished from a long stage absence, and a comeback was planned. The Colonel now steered Elvis away from live rock and towards the more mellow sound.

Yet the King still had an amazing rapport with audiences, especially in his most frequent venue, Las Vegas. But keeping up with a grueling schedule increased his reliance on prescription drugs. His elaborate rhinestone and studded outfits added as much as 35 pounds to his already bulky weight. Priscilla left him in 1972, and several scandals ensued, ranging from paternity suits to rumors of drug orgies. In private, he shot TVs during his frequent rages and yet publicly displayed a legendary kindness, often buying Cadillacs for complete strangers.

When Elvis died from an accidental drug overdose, orders poured in for eight million of his records. His total number of album sales rose to one billion, the highest of any recording artist to date. Elvis' influence on popular culture continues to grow. Musicians, including **Little Richard**, **Johnny Cash**, and **Bruce Springsteen**, have released tribute songs and albums. More recently, the memory of the King has shaped movies like *Mystery Train* (1989), a dreamy exploration of the Elvis phenomena.

**Elvis Presley.**

# TRIVIA QUIZ & GAMES

1. Which folk heroes were thought to have miraculously survived their deaths? (See nos. 9, 20, and 76)

2. Which folk heroes are believed by many to have faked their deaths? (See nos. 62, 67, 98, and 100)

3. Name the important writers, poets, and folklorists who were also folk heroes. (See nos. 3, 5, 45, 47, 56, and 85)

4. Name two thinkers whose visionary writings shaped modern thought. (See nos. 4 and 23)

5. Name eight folk heroes who many feel never lived. (See nos. 2, 3, 9, 10, 11, 12, 15, 18, and 32)

6. Which criminal's exploits were sung to peasants by bards? (See no. 15) Name four entries whose subjects were perceived to be modern versions of him. (See nos. 62, 67, 77, and 92)

7. Who helped lead the Third Crusade? (See no. 16)

8. Which two unlucky queens were beheaded? (See nos. 26 and 39)

9. Which two hated folk heroes became the basis for great horror novels? (See nos. 21 and 37)

10. Which sixteenth century seer predicted several major events that would occur after his death, including some still slated to happen? (See no. 25)

11. Name two criminals who have annual celebrations in their honor. (See nos. 27 and 98)

12. Name two religious figures that are at the center of major holidays. (See nos. 7 and 8)

13. Which three folk heroes are regarded as some of the greatest lovers the world has ever known? (See nos. 6, 34 and 73)

14. Name two celebrated American showmen and two of their most famous performers. (See nos. 49, 61, 57, and 68)

15. Which two folk heroes became the basis of major American ballads? (See nos. 59 and 70)

16. Which stage actress is celebrated as the greatest of her kind? (See no. 60) Which magician? (See no. 75) Which opera singer? (See no. 74)

17. One enigmatic movie star portrayed two other folk heroes in her films. Who is she and who did she portray? (See no. 90)

18. Who was the most decorated soldier of World War II? (See no. 95)

19. Name three folk heroes who were the subjects of scandal after their deaths. (See nos. 83, 88, and 96)

20. Which folk heroes are at the core of intriguing mysteries? (See nos. 24, 50, 86, and 89)

21. Which three performers were elevated to a god-like status after their deaths? (See nos. 96, 99, and 100)

22. Which film stars immortalized Antony and Cleopatra? (See no. 6)

23. Which film stars established today's romantic image of Bonnie and Clyde? (See no. 92)

24. What 19th century British poet wrote of King Arthur and his knights as well as Lady Godiva? (See nos. 9, 10, 11, and 12) His American counterpart wrote of Hiawatha, John and Priscilla Alden, and Paul Revere. Who was he? (See nos. 19, 29, and 36)

# INDEX

110